Dear Wendel —

Hope you enjoy —

Best Wishes —

Ron

TWIN TALES

Ronald Allbee

Print ISBN: 978-1-09834-833-5
eBook ISBN: 978-1-09834-834-2

TWIN'S TALE

DEDICATED to my parents who had little and sacrificed so we might survive, learn, serve and enjoy adventures throughout our lives

TABLE OF CONTENTS

TIMELINE

JAN 9, 1945	BIRTH AT BRATTLEBORO MEMORIAL
SEPT 1951	BROOKLINE GRADE SCHOOL
SEPT 1959	LELAND AND GRAY SEMINARY
SEPT 1963	UNIVERSITY OF VERMONT
AUG 1967	OCS NAVY, NEWPORT, R.I.
DEC 1967	NUCLEAR WEAPONS TRAINING
MAR 1968	USS AMERICA (CVA-66)
APRIL 10, 68	AMERICA SAILS TO VIETNAM
NOV 69	DEPART NAVY
JAN 70	GRAD SCHOOL, CONNECTICUT
SEPT 72	VT. LEGISLATIVE COUNCIL
OCT 74	DEPUTY CMR VERMONT AGRICULTURE
JUNE 75	ACTING CMR OF AGRICULTURE
JAN 76	DEPUTY CMR OF AGRICULTURE
MAY 78	VT. DIRECTOR OF ENERGY
DEC 80	ENERGY SOLUTIONS
DEC 82	NORWICH UNIVERSITY
	GREEN MOUNTAIN FEDERATION
OCT 84	STRAW AND HAY, BRATTLEBORO
	SENATOR PATRICK LEAHY
AUG 86	COMMISSIONER OF AGRICULTURE
DEC 90	SENATOR PATRICK LEAHY
	CHEESE TRADERS
	BLOCKHOUSE BED AND BRK
	CANADIAN DAIRY INDUSTRY
DEC 95	BUSINESS CONSULTING
JULY 2004	SKINMART DERMATOLOGY
JULY 2008	HEARTCARE CONSULTANTS
JULY 2016	BUSINESS CONSULTING

INTRODUCTION

Twin Tales is a collection of short stories and adventures of a twin boy born into poverty in a small Vermont town in the 1940s. These stories capture the times and experiences of a twin as he travels from a small Vermont town of 104 people to the larger world of Montpelier, Washington, D.C., and beyond! The book is titled *TWIN TALES* and captures experiences moving from a farm in a small Vermont town to government positions, businesses, and finally, to helping start and manage several medical practices.

My identical twin and I were born into a struggling farming and forestry family in Brookline, a small town in Southern Vermont. Prior to the Civil War, it was a flourishing town with two inns, two churches, a blacksmith shop, lumber mills, and many farms. Like other Vermont towns, the population decreased following the civil war as the tired and hardworking population found better lands to the west. When we were born, Brookline had a population of 102 plus 2 by the birth of my twin and myself.

We grew up on a small dairy farm with a maple sugar orchard and a lumber mill. My father and uncle also operated a small construction company. Our relatives and neighbors returned from World War II and the Korean War and were re-establishing themselves. We learned about government in our town meetings. Our schools were small and our teachers strict. Not only did we receive our education in our schools; we also received an education in the surrounding environment. The rivers and streams were full of fish, and the woods were full of wild animals. We did not worry about locking our doors, for everyone was trusted. We helped those who fell on misfortune, for it was the neighborly thing to do. We were poor and did not know it, for an abundance of food surrounded us, and most everyone we knew was poor like us! The people we encountered helped shape our character. While our high school was poor and possessed few facilities, the teachers were committed and provided a wonderful education. We learned we would be treated as we treated others. One did not take a day's work lightly, and one's word was as good as a written commitment. It was from this background I entered the world of college, service, and finally, positions taking me from government to business

The following short snippets provide insight into some of the people and situations I encountered.

CHAPTER 1

TWINS

BEARING twins today is not as an uncommon occurrence as it was in years prior. A woman has about a 32 in 1,000 chance of having twins, but only a 3 in 1,000 chance of identical twins. Through the centuries, the overwhelming response to twins has been to regard them either as unnatural and monstrous or divine deserving of worship. Born as identical twins, we were indeed considered quite unique. Being an identical twin is a wonderful experience and has often not been properly explained to non-twins. Throughout life, you are compared and displayed for all to see. Many find identical twins confusing and react strangely to this uniqueness of nature. Being an identical twin presented us with great opportunities to foil those less twin knowledgeable and to experience instances where we were often confused. In school, we were not called Ron or Rog, only Twin. Our parents often could not tell us apart. When one misbehaved, we both ran for they often simply punished the first one caught. My sympathies were always with the caged animals at the zoo there for other's viewing. We were treated as caged twins and gawked at and pointed to throughout life. People tend to assume because you look alike you are alike! This is simply not true. Identical looks do not beget identical personalities. Although we graduated with similar grades in high school and college, we were not similar. We looked similar and often acted similar, but we differed in many ways. As an identical twin, we struggled to establish our own identity. Finally realizing this dream when we graduated from college and went into separate branches of the U.S. military during the Vietnam War.

MY PARENT'S SURPRISE!

IT was the end of World War II, and my parents were a poor Vermont farming family with a 7-year-old boy and a 6-year-old girl. My mother was expecting another child and my father was earning hardly enough money to support the existing family. Ultrasounds or other devices did not exist to show a woman she was expecting more than one child or even the sex of the child. On a cold January night, my mother went into labor at the Brattleboro Memorial Hospital. Early in the morning of January 9, Dr. Otis, our family physician, delivered a son (me). After the delivery, Dr. Otis informed my mother there was another baby and she was not yet done delivering. Approximately thirty minutes later, another baby boy arrived. It was the beginning of an identical twin relationship which would reward and challenge us. It is a relationship difficult to explain to others. We would tell people we were proof cloning should be prohibited! The total cost for our delivery was a mere $61.00. It was $11.00 more than my father brought home in a week!

CONFUSION

I JUST PREPARED YOU FOR AN OPERATION!

ONE late weekday evening when we were about twelve, Roger was experiencing pains in his side. My parents rushed him to Brattleboro Memorial Hospital where he was diagnosed with appendicitis. It was late evening, and they had taken him into a room to prepare for surgery. With nothing to do while my parents were waiting, I went looking for my brother's room. As I was approaching the room, a nurse came to me and said, "I just prepared you for surgery, how did you get out of bed?" I told her I was feeling better and had changed my mind. She immediately went charging into the room only to see my brother lay prepared for surgery.

I AM RESIGNING!

THE American Cheese Society annual meeting was held in Burlington, Vermont when my twin brother was serving as Vermont's secretary of agriculture. He attended several sessions of the meetings and addressed the national group. My wife and I were attending a Saturday night reception with good friends. I was standing in line to check in and a young man came up and said, "Mr. Secretary, how are you tonight." I told him I was not very well, and he asked why. I said I just returned from the television station, and he would see the news tomorrow. He asked about the news. I said I announced my resignation as secretary. He was a staff member of the agency and it did not take him long to tell the other members of the staff my brother, the secretary, resigned as secretary of agriculture.

DIFFERENT MILKMEN FOR FATHERS

OUR mother drove to Brattleboro grocery shopping every Friday. Brattleboro was fifteen miles from our house, and a trip a week was the most we could afford. She purchased her weekly groceries at the A&P store located on Main Street. She often had other errands and let us visit the many stores on the street. We went into Woolworths, and two clerks asked if we were identical twins. We were amused when people asked such a silly question, for we were obviously identical. We came up with a very appropriate response. We told the clerks we were not identical and had different milkmen for fathers. It always caused an interesting response.

SHOE STORE WITH UNIQUE EQUIPMENT

BAKER'S shoe store was located on Elliot Street in Brattleboro. My mother took us there to buy shoes. While one of us was fitted with shoes, the other would play with the store equipment. They had a foot x-ray machine. When you placed your foot under the machine, it would show an x-ray of all your foot bones. What a marvelous way to examine your foot. The store owners and users were not aware of the danger of x-ray's in the early 1950's.

HE IS ALWAYS IN TROUBLE!

I was in Telluride, Colorado on a fishing trip in 2013 when I went into a cooperative art store. Our fishing guide was an artist with his art exhibited at the cooperative. I noticed the cooperative manager watching me as I viewed the exhibits. She finally asked me if I knew Roger Allbee. She said I looked like the person she knew. I said I was often confused with the person and was aware he lived in Vermont and was always in trouble with the authorities. A strange look came over her face! I finally told her he was my identical twin brother. She was the cousin of my brother's wife.

CALL THE GOVERNOR

MY twin brother was serving as Secretary of Agriculture under Governor Jim Douglas. A new administrative assistant was assisting him. Roger was not in his office one morning and I walked in and asked her to call the Governor. At first, she thought I was Roger. She quickly replied, "if I had not just talked to him on the phone in Southern Vermont I would!

HE WAS DRINKING BEER IN GERMANY!

ROGER was commissioned in the army and spent his Vietnam years in Germany assisting the British Army. I, on the other hand, spent many months on a carrier off the coast of North Vietnam. He told people I did not really serve in Vietnam because I was not on land but cruised the waters offshore. North of White River Junction , Vermont on Interstate 89, a rest area is named in honor of those who served and died in Vietnam. On my first stop, I approached the service desk and looked at the book listing service members. I noted my brother's name in the book and told the people monitoring the desk his name should be removed as he did not serve in the conflict. They informed me they were service members who served during the Vietnam era. Those who actually served in Vietnam were listed on the marble wall. I said if his name was on the wall it should be removed. Fortunately, only my name was inscribed on the wall.

WHY NOT ME!

THERE are things twins learn about each other later in life. Much later, he told me about his religious experience. He told me of the experience after his heart attack. When he was twelve, God came to him and told him to devote himself to God and become a minister. Later, when I was serving as commissioner of agriculture, I asked one of my minister friends why God did not come to me? My good minister friend said, "Ron, doesn't that tell you something!"

DID YOU SEE FIRE!

MOST of us read or hear about near-death experiences. My father died from liver cancer in the fall of 1988. During the winter of 1988-1989, my brother and his wife were cross-country skiing with a church group in Ludlow, Vermont. While skiing, Roger passed out and was encouraged to ski back to the lodge. One skier went ahead and called an ambulance. At the lodge, he insisted he ride to the hospital in his car, but the person skiing with him insisted he ride in the ambulance. We grew up with some of the ambulance crew, and Roger started talking with them about other acquaintances when his heart stopped. Fortunately, it was a well-trained ambulance crew, and after fourteen minutes, while maintaining oxygen to his brain, they were able to restart his heart. He was still being treated and evaluated when I arrived at the hospital. His wife Anne and I stayed in the hospital all night while he was stabilized. We were invited to his room early the next morning. He said he suffered a heart attack. I said we were aware of the attack, but I wanted to know if "he saw fire!" He said he did not see the fire. He saw our father who told him it was not his time and he needed to return to help care for the rest of us.

Somewhat later, the hospital used his picture and information in a promotional advertisement. People who knew us would ask about Roger's health condition. I would explain, telling them his heart had stopped for fourteen minutes. They always asked if he suffered brain damage. I always told them I could not tell the difference!

Governors and Twins

<><><><><><><><><><><><><><><><><><><><><><><><><>

YOU ARE NOT RON!

Governor Snelling was unaware of my twin brother when I served as his deputy commissioner of agriculture. At the time, the agricultural department was mired in a Brucellosis outbreak making daily headlines. During my trials at the Vermont Department of Agriculture, the governor called me in one day to discuss the issues. He said, "Ron, I don't think you are a Republican, you are either an Independent or Democrat." I did not answer; it was not a statement one answered. The governor was a guest speaker at the Barre Republican Party dinner the same evening. By circumstance, my brother was taking tickets at the door. The governor arrived and the person he accused of not being a Republican is taking tickets. He said, "Ron, what the hell are you doing here tonight?" My brother told the governor he was not Ron, at which point the governor said, "Bullshit, prove it." So, my brother took out his wallet and showed the governor his I.D. Governor Snelling never mistook us again, nor did he ever accuse me of not being a Republican.

Gov. Richard A. Snelling (left) did a double-take Thursday night when he met Roger Allbee, twin brother of Ronald Allbee, Vermont's deputy agriculture commissioner, at a Barre Town Republican Committee covered-dish supper. At first Snelling had trouble believing there could be two Allbees, until the smiling Roger pulled out some identification for the governor to see. The latter Allbee is an employee of the Vermont Environmental Conservation Agency and is a Barre Town School Board member. (Racz photo)

CUFF HIM

I was at an agricultural dinner with Governor Kunin. I always provided her police escorts with dinner and came to know all the state police escorts. At one dinner, one of the policemen came up and said, "Ron, do you know there is someone here tonight who looks exactly like you?" I said I did and was having many difficulties with the person. I asked him to cuff him and arrest him as soon as possible! I finally told the officer the truth before my brother was arrested.

CONGRESSMAN JEFFORDS AND TWINS

I serving as Vermont energy director in the late 1970s. Commissioner of Agriculture William Darrow asked for a recommendations for deputy commissioner. I recommended George Dunsmore who was serving as Congressman Jeffords' agricultural aide. George and I were classmates at the University of Vermont, and George had an in-depth knowledge of Vermont agriculture. Bill Darrow hired George, and shortly thereafter, I received a call from George inquiring if I might be interested in working for Congressman Jeffords. I recently assumed the energy position and was not anxious to make another move. However, I told George I would be happy to meet with the congressman in Washington to discuss the position. I traveled to D.C to discuss the position with Jim Jeffords. After much consideration, my family and I decided we were not prepared to make a move. I informed the congressman of my decision and told him I had a twin brother who might be interested. Roger interviewed and was offered the Washington position I turned down.

CARRYING TWO BUSINESS CARDS… ONE FOR FRIENDLY GROUPS AND ONE FOR ANGRY GROUPS

I was serving as Vermont's commissioner of agriculture, and my twin brother was a vice president with the New England Farm Credit Service. He was always well received when he spoke to farmers. I, on the other hand, often dealt with the farm groups under difficult circumstances. He provided money and credit. I provided a host of regulations. Thus, I would carry both business cards. If I encountered an angry group, I would invite them to call and hand out his business cards. A friendly group would of course receive my business cards.

CHAPTER 2

PARENTS

IF we are fortunate, our parents are our heroes. My father left school after the eighth grade when his mother died in childbirth. He was a math whiz and could fix anything or invent any tool. My mother left school after her sophomore year in high school following the death of her father. Both survived, loved their children, and encouraged each to further their education. They made do with very little and had a large pool of friends.

My father was a Vermont humorist. He always had a joke or a way of finding humor in an event or action. My mother was quieter and did not like to take a position or voice her views publicly. However, at home, my mother was the disciplinarian, and my father was the person who would walk away from admonishing us.

Father

∞∞

DOMINATED BY A WOMAN FOR 50 YEARS

I was serving as Governor Kunin's commissioner of agriculture when my father was dying from bone and liver cancer. Cancer had attacked the nerves to his eyes leaving him unable to see. Madeline Kunin was running for re-election, and I was helping my father fill out his absentee ballot. He had always been an ardent Republican, and I knew it would be difficult to convince him to vote for my boss. I said, "Dad, can't you vote for her so I can keep my job?" He said, "I've been dominated by a woman for fifty years, and I'll be damned if I am going to vote for one." It was not how he felt about women, but it was his way of telling me that he would never vote for a Democrat.

DIDN'T LOOK RIGHT WHEN YOU WERE BORN!

MY father his father, grandfather and great grandfather were Republicans. They were moderate Republicans and believed in helping those truly in need and spending public money as though it was their own. They also believed in the honesty of those who led. It was a different Republican Party than exists today. My father was proud of his Yankee integrity and his belief in the Republican Party. My older brother worked for the Eugene McCarthy's Democratic presidential campaign in Connecticut, and I was working for a Democratic governor. I asked my father how he managed to have two Republicans and two Democrats in the family with his Republican heritage. He said, "When you and your older brother were born, I looked at each of you and knew something was wrong."

REGRETS

DAD was in Dartmouth Hitchcock in Hanover, New Hampshire receiving radiation treatment for his cancer. His life was ebbing away and he was in the oncology ward for treatment. A young Episcopal priest in training was going through the ward talking to the patients. He came to my father who was in his last stages of the cancer. He asked my father, "Mr. Allbee, do you have any regrets in life for which you wish to be forgiven?" My father responded, "My only regret is that I have no regrets!" The priest walked away confused and bewildered.

CLEANING OUT THE CELLAR

MY father, my grandfather, and his brother were collectors. They never threw anything away and never protected anything from the weather. You could never tell when you might need something, so why throw it out, they reasoned. I believe the habit came from my grandfather who was a reluctant farmer and down deep just didn't want to worry about anything but reading a good book or dealing with legislative issues. I can't remember my grandfather ever repairing the farmhouse or the barn. When he was done with a car, he parked it in the back forty. My father filled our cellar with his tools and other collections. He always knew where an item was located, but the rest of us would hunt for it for hours. Once a year, our mother would tire of the mess in the cellar and tell us to clean it out. She would direct us to fill up one of the dump trucks with the collection and dispose of it before my father came home. We knew destroying my father's prized possessions would enrage him. We started the disposal as my mother directed. We timed our efforts to my father's return. We knew when our father would come home and planned to be about one-third of the way into the project when he arrived. He told us to immediately unload the truck and discontinue our efforts. My mother would again direct us to clean the cellar in another six months.

CAN THE CAR MAKE IT OVER PUTNEY MOUNTAIN?

IN the 1950s, it was not uncommon for car salesmen to bring cars to you. My father loved Chevys, and one day, he took us to Greenfield, Massachusetts to look at the cars at the Chevy dealer. My father kicked a lot of tires, and the salesperson really tried to sell him a car. Unfortunately, dad gave him his home address in Brookline, never thinking the salesperson would drive so far with a car. One day, he appeared at the lumber mill with a 1952 power glide Chevy. It was one of those new automatic cars, and he told my father the car was able to perform as well as a standard on any hill. That is when he made his greatest mistake. My father asked his friend Cal Dean to join them, and they set out for a trip up and down Putney Mountain with its hairpin turns. My father put the car through every test possible over the mountain. They returned to the mill, and the salesperson was seen driving off with smoke coming out of the car. I am sure the automatic transmission was not up to the mountain trial. The salesperson never showed up at the mill again.

WHEN MY NAME APPEARS IN THE PAPERS, I WILL NOT BE AROUND TO READ IT

MY father was quite a humorous. He said when his name appeared in the paper, he would not be around to read it. He was quite right, for he was not around to read his obituary.

THREE BRANCHES OF GOVERNMENT

MY father left school at the end of the eighth grade to work on his family farm. He excelled in mathematics, could figure anything mechanical and invented many devices. However, his grasp of political science and government was limited to the town meeting, voting for governor, and voting Republican for president. Royal was our insurance agent and also a representative to the legislature from the town of Townshend. In those days, each town sent a representative to Montpelier. We were either sophomores or juniors in High School and sat listening to Royal and my father talk about politics. My father brought up some issue, and finally, Royal said, "Harlan, you must understand, there are three branches of government, the legislative of which I am a member, the executive, and the judicial. Unfortunately, my powers in the legislative branch are not complete and can be checked by the judicial branch. Sometimes how the executive interprets a bill is not the same as it is written." We understood that my father's grasp of government was limited, and he was receiving an education from Royal.

DAD AND PEOPLE ON RETREAT FARM… IF YOU PLAY WITH YOURSELF

THE Retreat Dairy Farm was located on Route 30 as you entered Brattleboro from the north. The Retreat was a treatment facility where they treated many disorders. Many of the residents were severely handicapped. During the 1950s, residents at the retreat provided labor to the farm. My father delivered lumber to Brattleboro, and we often rode in the truck. When we passed the farm, we saw many handicapped residents walking toward the farm to help with the chores. My father often pointed to them and told us if we "played with ourselves" we would look like the handicapped residents!

SAYING GRACE

DAD was not a religious man who attended church and talked about God. His church was in the woods, streams, and among the animals. He believed in God, but his God was in the environment. Whenever we had guests for dinner, my mother would insist he say grace. It was an uncomfortable time for him, yet he tried his best. One time my great-aunt joined us at Thanksgiving dinner and my mother insisted he say grace. Dad looked at the turkey and said, "God bless this carcass and may it taste as good as it looks!" I thought my great-aunt would faint, but she also understood my father's humor.

BPOE AND ESSO

DAD would always answer our questions as to the meaning of a word or initials. When we passed the BPOE building in Brattleboro and asked what it meant, he replied with, "Biggest Pricks on Earth." When we asked what the ESSO gas stations signs meant, he said, "Every Sucker Stops Once!"

DAD AND NYSTROM'S PARTY

EVERY summer, my mother, her sister, my cousin, and us kids would spend two weeks in Cape Cod at my aunt's house. We had a wonderful time swimming, fishing, and often, waiting on the two ladies while they shopped. One summer when we came home, we were told about a party at the Nystrom's house where they entertained townspeople. The Nystrom girls were our classmates, and they divulged much of what went on at the party. I guess my father had a wonderful time and really enjoyed himself. From that point on whenever he threatened to punish us, we would say, "Dad, we will tell mother about the Nystrom party." He would immediately stop. I think he thought we knew more about the party than we really did… but the threat served us well.

Mother

⬦⬦⬦⬦⬦

ELECTRICITY

MOTHER talked about when electricity came to Brookline. Prior to electricity, they read with oil lamps and utilized oil lamps when working in the barn. Their first lightbulb was 20 watts, and my mother said it was quite bright. They did not put electricity in the barn because they were afraid of fire; they preferred oil lamps!

MOTHER'S DEER

MOTHER was not a deer hunter. She cooked the venison for my father and the rest of us and hated the meat. She would not pick up a gun. Although we did not post no hunting signs on our land, we did place signs around the property instructing hunters not to hunt or fire around the house, as it was a safety zone. My mother was in the yard one day and noticed some hunters stopped with their guns aimed directly toward the side of our house. Before she could say anything, one of their guns discharged, and she saw a deer near the house fall to the ground. She was disgusted by their disregard for the safety zone and charged and directed them to move on. They insisted on taking the deer. But due to my mother's anger and her threat to call the authorities, they moved on without their deer. My father returned home from a day of hunting and found my mother's deer. Without holding a gun or firing a shot, my mother had bagged a deer.

MOTHER'S LETTER TO THE EDITOR

WE graduated from the University of Vermont and were spending the summer in Brookline before going into the service. He a second lieutenant in the army, and I about to enter Navy Officer Candidate School (OCS) in Newport, Rhode Island. There was a Vietnam War and every day the news carried headlines about troop deaths in that Asian country. One day, the *Brattleboro Reformer*, the local paper, carried the headline about a local soldier who killed a Viet Cong. We thought making any death a headline, even an enemy combatant, was not appropriate. Since we were in the service, we knew we could not write a letter to the editor under our own names. So, we drafted a letter to the editor outlining our views and sent it under my mother's name. My mother probably shared our opinion, but she was a person who never wanted to see her name in print and would never publicly voice an opinion. On the day the letter appeared in the paper, she received calls congratulating her on her written opinion. Not only was she embarrassed, but she was mad at us. I think she was ready to send us off to the service at that moment, even to Vietnam!

In The July 31st issue of the Reformer I was dismayed to see that you carried a descriptive story of a local soldier killing a "Viet Cong," or as he is commonly called "Charlie." You seem to neglect the human element— soldiers are not born killers. The normal human neither wants to is proud of taking another human life.

We have heard the pro's and con's of the Viet Nam war from the informed and the ill-informed—from these sources we have tried to draw our own conclusions. As civilians we are able to protest and express our feelings toward the war.

The soldier also draws his own conclusions, but as a soldier he can not and must not protest against what he has been called upon to support. At times he must kill, but he is not killing the individual, he is killing a part of that which threatens him. I can not really believe that the young soldier was proud of what he had done. It was something which he did in the line of duty.

Many of the so called Viet Cong are local peasants conscripted by the communists. They have neither heard of Marx or Engles nor understand the ideological

difference between democracy and Communism. They fight for the food which they can give their families. They must kill or be killed as we must kill or be killed. They are not animals which lack a means of communication. After reading such reports I can only question the quality of the news which we are receiving.

CHASING A PIG OFF THE FRONT LAWN

WE traveled to a pig farm in Putney, Vermont to buy three pigs to raise behind our house. Two of the pigs started growing rapidly, but the third pig was obviously a runt and stayed small. The little pig was always getting out from under the pen, going up to the house, and following my mother around the yard. When she was hanging clothes on the line, the pig would startle her by appearing behind her! He was truly a smart and friendly little pig. My mother did not take kindly to having a little pig following her around and was seen one day chasing it around the yard with a broom. I think she was afraid of what the neighbors would say about her, Jessie, having a pig as a friend!

DON'T COME BACK IF YOU ARE GOING TO TELL ME THAT AGAIN

DR. Backus, a very popular and caring doctor in Townshend, Vermont, was my mother's doctor. He often visited her during her last days. On one visit, she asked if she were dying. Dr. Backus said, "Yes, Jessie, you are dying." As he was leaving, he asked her if she would like him to come back and visit again. She said, "No, not if you are going to tell me that again!"

MOTHER'S MEMORY AND LAST DAYS IN HELL

MY mother was a resident of a senior housing facility in Townshend, Vermont. Her mind had frayed, but she still knew her immediate family. I was living in Florida at the time and visited her every five to six weeks. Toward the end, I would tell her I was Ron. She would insist I was Roger since he lived nearby and made daily visits. I would again insist I was Ron, and she would finally say, "Well, it really doesn't matter does it?" I would respond, "Mother, it really does not matter!" During her last few weeks, she showed every sign of accepting death and even sang farewell songs to people. One day, my brother was leaving after a visit and said, "Mother, I will see you tomorrow." She said, "You may not as I may be in hell tomorrow." It was a cold and wintery day. My brother asked why she would be in hell. She said, "It is warmer down there!!"

MOTHER AND KITTENS ON SLEEPING BAG

MY dear mother loved animals. After many of our cats had kittens, I think she came to the conclusion we had too many cats. My brother, a friend, and I were camping near the stream in front of our house. One of our pregnant cats birthed kittens on my sleeping bag during the night. We told our mother about the experience at breakfast the next morning. While we were eating breakfast, my mother ventured to the tent and threw the kittens into the small pond in the stream. Unfortunately for my mother, the mother cat watched and quickly rescued all the kittens from the stream. Those kittens had a second life and lived to adulthood. It was the end of my mother's cat extermination experiments.

CHAPTER 3

PEOPLE

Mr. Ed!

◇◇◇◇◇◇

ED was a bachelor living with his brother and sister in the northern part of Brookline. Ed served as a caretaker for several summer properties. He drove an old 1942 Chevy ¾-ton pickup around town no more than 30 mph. Ed and his pal, Hoyt Marsh, were always parked next to the Brookline/Newfane Bridge late every afternoon. After a day's work, they would be drinking their beer and telling their stories.

We turned sixteen and were looking to purchase our first vehicle. My father learned Ed was upgrading to another pickup and thought perhaps his old pickup might be for sale. One evening, we drove to Ed's house and asked if he wanted to sell his truck. He said he would sell it to us for $18.00, but since he had yet to take possession of his newer vehicle, we would need to wait a week to take possession. He told us to come back the following week. We went back to see Ed the following week with our $18.00. We told him we had the money for his pickup, and he said, "Can't do it!" We were dismayed, and he said "No, I went to the junkyard today, and all they would give me for the pickup was $12.00, so that is all I will take from you boys." We paid him the $12.00 and drove off with our first vehicle. We named the vehicle Mr. Ed in his honor. There was also a T.V. show with a talking horse called Mr. Ed, so there was some confusion with the name.

Mr. Ed Proved to be quite a vehicle… it drove and functioned like a World War II tank. The one windshield wiper worked intermittingly. The front window only partially opened, and one of us would stick his hand out and move the wiper with his free hand while the other drove. On cold and icy days, it was nearly impossible to see as you drove. The tires were always bald taken from my father's cast-off pile behind our mill. The vehicle had no directional lights, and if you were turning, you stuck your arm out and give a turn signal. The heater made a strange noise and blew cold air

When we turned the key off and on as we drove, the motor would explode and a red fireball would exit the exhaust. We used the option when we wanted to awaken a household at night. Eventually, the motor started using oil and a 5 gallon can of oil would only last a week. Any car behind us drove in peril of being enclosed in a white cloud of smoke. Finally, the motor gave out and my father helped us perform a motor job installing new rings and valves.

HOYT MARSH

HOYT was a Vermont farmer with a wry with, intellectual curiosity and a well-defined taste for good liquor. His humor was honed from the Vermont hills. He looked every bit a stereotype Vermont farmer: short in statue, stooped shoulders, a handlebar mustache and a twinkle in his eyes. He loved a good story and could spin a good yarn. His intellect and curiosity were such he was never underestimated. He was an expert with dynamite and the making of hard cider. The following stories relate to Hoyt and his wife Minnie, who served as town clerk. She actually ran the town. She was so accomplished the Selectmen thought they ran the town. During deer season hunters would check their deer at Minnie's. She could estimate the weight of the deer within 5 pounds.

WHERE IS THE CENTER OF BROOKLINE?

ONE day, Hoyt was standing outside his house located in the center of Brookline. There was no town center, but if you cut the town in half, Hoyt and Minnie's house was in the center. A car pulled up and the driver asked Hoyt if he could direct him to the center of Brookline. Hoyt slowly pulled on his mustache, looked both up and down the road, and finally, said, "Guess, by God, you're in it!"

HOLEY KNIGHT AND SILENT KNIGHT

HOYT'S neighbors were a couple named Knight. Mr. Knight was a woodworker who made items for sale. His work often had holes routed out for decorative purposes. Mrs. Knight was very quiet and thin and virtually silent. Hoyt referred to the couple as Holey Knight and Silent Knight. Mrs. Knight was so thin Hoyt said, "She could look down the neck of a bottle with both eyes." There was an old church next to the Knight's property. Hoyt and some friends wanted to buy it and turn it into a tavern. The Knights were so opposed they bought the church and burned it to the ground.

GUESS BY GOD I'M A REPUBLICAN

THE minister visited Hoyt one day. Hoyt was sitting in a rocking chair near the window as the minister talked. They shared some stories before the minister came to his purpose for the visit. He asked, "Mr. Marsh, what denomination are you?" Hoyt thought for a while and said, "Guess, by God, you can call me a Republican."

ROUGH ROAD OVER PUTNEY MOUNTAIN

A dirt road leads over the Putney Mountain from Brookline to Putney. At places, it gets very steep and rough. There is also a turn on the mountain road referred to as the "Hairpin Turn." Hoyt drove a pickup truck with a dog that often rode in the back. Daily, Hoyt would drive to the Newfane store owned by Earl Morse and his mother. Earl asked Hoyt if he had driven over the Putney Mountain Road and if it was rough. Hoyt said he had recently driven up the road, and it was, "So rough his dog was jerking off in the back."

DRY PLUCKING CHICKENS WHEN ALIVE

HOYT was famous for his hard cider. After cider has finished fermentation, it is drawn off. The keg is then emptied of all its mash. Mash is left over from the alcohol-making process. One day as Hoyt was imbibing his cider after tending the finished keg, he dumped the mash on the ground. He then returned to his comfortable seat overlooking yard and was enjoying his new hard cider. He looked out and noticed his chickens had consumed the mash and were lying in the yard – apparently dead. Being a frugal Vermonter, he did not want to miss what was possibly dinner and lunchmeat. He went out and dry plucked the chickens and returned to his house to prepare for more chicken processing. Probably half drunk, he returned to the chickens and discovered they were returning to life – without feathers. They had been drunk, not dead.

FILTERING HARD CIDER

MY father and Zeke were Brookline cemetery commissioners. Zeke loved to make his own home brew and was also famous for his parties. It was a warm summer day, and my father and Zeke agreed to meet in the cemetery to discuss some lot issues. Zeke brought some of his hard cider and passed it around. They were standing near Hoyt's grave. Zeke turned toward it and said, "Hoyt, would you like this straight or would you like me to drink it, strain it, and then give it to you?" Zeke continued, "I know you, Hoyt. You would drink it first. Zeke took a drink, opened his pants, and pissed on Hoyt's grave.

WE DON'T HAVE GOOD NEIGHBORS!

THE town's selectmen were at Minnie and Hoyt's house discussing town business with Minnie. Hoyt was always present, either nodding quietly and rocking in his chair or telling stories. He turned to Minnie and said,

"Minnie, why did we never have any good neighbors?" Minnie replied, "Why, Hoyt, we had many good neighbors." "Well then," said Hoyt, "why did we never have any children?"

TRYING TO MAKE BROOKLINE WET

BROOKLINE was a very small community in the fifties and sixties. It had 104 residents, including women and children. The annual town meeting was held in the round schoolhouse. It was a small building ,but large enough to hold the town meetings. Minnie and the town moderator, who was my grandfather, would sit up front. Hoyt always sat in the front row, and one of the items always on the ballot was: "Will the town of Brookline approve the sale of malt beverages in town?" The vote was by Australian ballot in secret, and Hoyt was always the first to complete his ballot and put it in the box. The count was always two in favor and the remainder opposed. It was well known Hoyt and Ed McPhail cast the only votes in favor. Since there was no retail outlet in town, we never knew what they had planned if the vote was in favor of liquor sales.

INSUFFICIENT EQUIPMENT

THE Siepman family summered in a house directly across from Hoyt and Minnie's. Dr. Siepman was a professor at Harvard and was friendly with such prominent luminaries as Dr. Kenneth Galbraith, Edward R Murrow and Alistair Cook. In the summer they swam in a pool in Grassy Brook adjacent to the field on their property. Sometimes, they swam in the nude. One day, the Galbraiths were visiting with their long-term maid, Emily. Hoyt thought he would sneak up on the pool and watch Emily swim in the nude. She saw Hoyt watching and came toward him and said, "Mr. Marsh, you don't have anything that would in any way provide me pleasure." Poor Hoyt.

IMPRESSING A SCHOLAR

HOYT was not beyond having a little fun, and whether he really read "Shakespeare," we will never know. However, he did know how to impress his neighbor who was a summer resident and liked visiting and listening to

Hoyt's stories. Dr. Siepman was educated in England and helped establish BBC T.V. He came to America and taught communications at Harvard. He often visited Hoyt, who did not have a high school education. Hoyt was sitting reading Shakespeare when Dr. Galbraith visited. While Hoyt was anything but stupid and may have actually read Shakespeare, it was more likely that he was having a little fun with his summer neighbor! Dr. Siepman went home to report that his neighbor, the Vermont farmer humorist, was a reader of Shakespeare.

PREDICTING SCHOOL AGE POPULATION

MINNIE served as Brookline's town clerk. While the elected selectmen thought they ran the town, the person most in charge was Minnie. If you wanted a fishing or hunting license, you visited Minnie. Her house was in the center of the town where town business was performed. Minnie had her finger on the pulse of the town. Brookline was served by a multi-party phone line, which meant you could listen in on other conversations. This occurred well before the present-day CIA's eavesdropping on conversations. If you needed to make a call, you asked the other party listening in to hang up. Minnie was often on the other end of the phone listening. Every year at town meeting, Minnie would report on the expected school attendance, sometimes two or three years in advance. Because she listened in on phone conversations, Minnie knew who was pregnant before they knew they were pregnant!

FIRST TOWN IN U.S. TO REPORT ELECTION RESULTS

IT was the 1952 presidential election and national networks were covering the results live. Edward R. Morrow was the anchor of one of the networks reporting results. He was a friend of Dr. Seipman who owned a house in Brookline adjacent to the Marsh's. Mr. Morrow purchased a TV for Dr. Siepman so he could view the results on live TV rather than the radio. So, as Dr. Siepman was watching, Mr. Morrow announced that Brookline, Vermont was the first town in the U.S. to report the results of the presidential election. I suspect it was 100% for Eisenhower. Minnie made sure Brookline, the summer home of Dr. Siepman was the first in the Nation.

WHAT IS PLAYING AT THE MOVIES?

PRIOR to reapportionment and the establishment of one man, one vote, each Vermont town sent a representative to Montpelier. The General Assembly only met once every two years to take care of the important business. The city of Burlington had no more influence in the state house than the town of Brookline with its 104 voters. The voters of Brookline elected a representative at the town meeting. The same was true for other towns. My grandfather was the representative in 1960, and he took the position seriously and studied all the proposed legislation. It was before welfare and state assistance, and sometimes a town would elect a person who was more in need of assistance the ability to represent a town. Every year, the elected representative would make a presentation to the citizens at a town meeting. One year, they elected a local farmer who needed assistance. When he came home to a town meeting to report on his service, he said he really could not report on the legislative session, but he did see all the movies in Montpelier.

GUESS BY GOD YOU DON'T KNOW WHO I AM!

HENRY Bush was a small dairy farmer who decided not to follow other farmers in installing bulk milk tanks in the 1960s. The Bushes were long-time residents of Brookline, and Henry brought up his family of three daughters and one son in a very small house with his parents. He served as head selectman of Brookline. Due to his father's deafness, Henry always spoke loudly. He was a very kind man who constantly chewed tobacco. When working with Henry, you wanted to stay out of range of the tobacco. Henry sold gravel from his pit and also worked for my father and uncle. He was a hard and tireless worker and a dear friend. However, Henry and his wife Olive did not travel much out of Vermont, and Brookline was the center of his universe. He took his position as head selectman seriously and considered his position very important. Henry was a Vermonter who considered every public dollar spent as money spent from his own pocket. I have several fond memories of Henry.

On one cold fall night we noticed a Massachusetts car parked near our house. In those days, there was not much vehicle traffic in Brookline, and all cars were accounted for quickly. The car stayed parked for a couple of days, and Henry and my father started looking for the owners. They finally traced the owners to a hunting camp on a hill which had been broken into for a few nights of recreation. The culprits were a young couple from the University of Massachusetts who decided they needed some excitement in their life. Henry and the selectmen did not know how to deal with the issue and decided to call the state police.

ONLY ONE WHO KNOWS WHAT SHE IS DOING

IN the 1960s, Wilbur Mills, the powerful chairperson of the House Ways and Means Committee, was caught frolicking in a wading pool in Washington with Fannie Fox, a known stripper. Our postman, Don Kent, had a wonderful sense of humor and said it was obvious that Ms. Fox was the only one that really knew what was going on in Washington!

COW MANURE MAKES MY FEET HEALTHY

GUY was my grandfather's neighbor farmer. We often helped Guy hay because he let us drive his small Allis Chambers tractor. It was a thrill to drive a vehicle at the age of twelve. Guy often walked around barefoot and could be seen cleaning out his gutters in his bare feet. In the 1950s, the small farmers cleaned their gutters by hand. Gutters were cement troughs behind the cows which collected the urine and manure.

TELEPHONE OPERATORS KNEW WHAT WAS HAPPENING!

THE switchboard for the local phone system was located on the first floor of the Odd Fellows Hall in Newfane. We toured the facility as cub scouts and watched the women operators respond to calls and place the connections in the appropriate slots. It would be some time before those operators were replaced by switching systems. One of the women who worked as an operator told me how they listened in on the calls. They would insert the connection halfway into the slot and would listen without either party knowing the conversation was heard. She said they knew everything happening in the community.

THE HORSE IS IN BETTER SHAPE THAN THE OWNERS

THE Ralph and Wendell lived on Newfane Hill in a rundown old farmhouse. Chickens ran free in the yard and a bony old horse chewed grass in the pasture. Weekly, they attached the bony old horse to their wagon and headed for town. It was their weekly visit to Morse's store to buy groceries and some beer. One of the men had a hook for a hand he either lost in a farming accident or during the war. They said little except nod their heads if you said hello. A new person moved into town. Upon seeing the brothers' horse, the person called the Animal Welfare Authorities. How could these men keep a horse in such condition? The authorities went to the farm to inspect and came back and said, "The horse is better fed than the brothers." They continued to drive to town once a week.

With a hook for one of his hands, he looked a little like Captain Hook. One day while working, his hook broke. They went down the road to visit the local welder, Cal, who immediately obliged. He asked him to put his hooked hand in a vice so he could weld the broken part back on. Cal was an expert welder, and the hand never broke again.

CREATING A DISTURBANCE ON NEWFANE COMMON

GUY Grout lived on Newfane Hill in a small farm adjacent to Grout's Pond. It was a thirty-acre pond where we often fished for bull pout (catfish). Guy was in his mid-eighties in the 1960s, and other than cutting some hay and tending some chickens, he was retired. He and his wife lived a quiet life on their farm. Every Fourth of July, Guy drove his old Jeep down to the Newfane Common wearing his WWI uniform. He would load his muzzleloader. At midnight, he touched off the gun and said, "God bless America." A crowd always formed to watch Guy shoot his muzzleloader and bless America. Things had gotten out of hand on the fourth and one year the sheriff's office notified everyone they would arrest those making noise or causing a disturbance on the common. Guy was notified he should not shoot his gun that year. We all gathered on the common on the 4th to see what would happen if Guy appeared. The sheriffs were there to arrest anyone causing a disturbance. At approximately 11:45 p.m., Guy drove up in his old Jeep, stepped out in his uniform and loaded his muzzleloader. At the appointed time—midnight—he shot the gun, said, "God bless America," got into his Jeep, and drove home. He continued this annual blessing until he could no longer drive!

WHAT TO DO WHEN KICKED OUT OF YOUR HOUSE

IT happened in Brookline before we were born and was a story handed down to my generation. Prior to the advent of welfare, people who owned houses and had no one to care for them as they aged sometimes signed their house over to a caretaker. The new owner agreed to care for the person and let him live in the property until death. Charlie, without any relatives to care for him, signed his house over to a man in Newfane with the understanding he could continue to live in the house until his death. After Charlie signed the document, the caretaker immediately evicted Charlie from his own house. All Charlie had was a wheelbarrow and the clothes on his back. He found a solution to his plight. He took off all his clothes and pushed the wheelbarrow around town naked. The residents thought he had lost his mind and committed him to the state mental institution in Waterbury, Vermont, where he had a warm bed and received three meals a day.

WON'T GET UP FOR ONE COW!

IT was a story handed down to me by my Calais friends. An East Montpelier dairy farmer who talked with a twinkle in his eye rented a small apartment to a young couple. One evening the couple went to the movies in Montpelier. On their way home they found one of his cows in the road. It was late at night and they knocked on the farmer's door to inform him of the cow. He came to the door in his nightshirt. They said, "Sir, one of your cows is in the road." He said, "Did you say one cow?" They answered in the affirmative. He said, "Guess I won't get up for one cow."

IT ALL DEPENDS

HAROLD served as president of the St. Albans Cooperative and was a large Maple producer in Franklin County, Vermont. A friend was sitting with Harold at a national dairy meeting when a farmer from a non-New England state asked Harold how much Maple syrup he produced. It was a normal question which Harold had become adept at answering. My friend who was the manager of the co-op watched in delight. Harold said, "It depends." The man said, "What does it depend on?" Harold said, "It depends on a lot of things. Sometimes, the snow is too high to hang all the buckets. Sometimes, the weather is not right to cause the sap to flow. Sometimes, the buds come out too early. Sometimes, the sap is not sweet enough." So, the farmer never got a straight answer.

PAINTING THE STATUE AT THE CATHOLIC CHURCH

OSCAR was my painting partner when I worked for Walt painting the interior and exteriors of houses. Walt would go out and find the jobs, and Oscar and others would perform the work. Walt would give few directions, as Oscar was the ultimate professional and knew all the tasks involved. Walt was contracted to paint the outside of the Catholic Church in Townshend, Vermont. He left Oscar to perform most of the work. While painting the exterior, Oscar noted the statue in the yard was rather dull and looked as though it needed a coat of paint. Oscar applied a nice coat of shiny white paint. Not too much later, he was told it was a fine Italian marble sculpture in its natural state and did not require paint. Oscar spent a day cleaning the paint from the statue.

WORLD WAR II HEROS

WE were born after World War II. The men and women who fought in those great battles were fathers, uncles, and neighbors. We thought little of what they had done when they dressed up in their uniforms on Memorial Day and participated in the activities. They said little about what they had done, but they took their valor and pride in their country seriously. There was my sister-in-law's father who was a retired Brigadier General in the Marine Corps who helped plan and participated in the battle of Iwo Jima. He came home and comforted himself with drinking and running a bar. There was the local hardware store owner who participated in the Bataan Death March. We knew little about his horrible experience until he died. My fishing and hunting partner, Julian Gomez, served as a turret gunner in a B-29 over Germany. We did not know of his exploits and the margin of his survival either until he died, for he told me little about his experiences. One of my uncles was wounded on D-Day. He was a sailor on an ammunition ship. Another uncle landed on D-Day, and his story follows. A professor at the University of Vermont also landed on D-Day and used his farm experience to gather apples for the troops when the Germans pinned them down without food for days.

USING AMBULATORY SOLDIERS

MY uncle Al was a Tennessee farm boy who was conscripted into the army and trained as a machine gunner. The night before the D-Day invasion, he and the other men on the ship went to a religious service. They knew many would die the next day. Al told his son the sky was lit up with bombardments the night before the landings. One of his fellow soldiers was calmly standing on the bow of the ship, and Al asked him how he could be so peaceful. The soldier told him he was prepared to meet his maker and was not afraid. The next day, they loaded onto the landing craft and started toward shore. They were taking shells when the landing craft door came down, and the soldier prepared to meet his maker took a bullet to the head and was the first of the troops in the craft to die. Al made it thru the

D-Day invasion and reached a small French town where he was wounded in the shoulder by a German soldier. He was sent to Belgium for rehab in an Army field hospital. While there the one of the retreating soldiers grabbed his coat and started dragging him to the rear. The next morning, Al awoke in a field hospital and was being fed blood from a soldier in the next cot. The soldier told him he was the one who saved Al and dragged him across the ice. Al thanked him and asked his name. He told Al his name was John. Al said he would name his firstborn son John. I told my cousin John he was lucky his name was not periwinkle, or he would be Periwinkle Smith.

FOOLING HIS BROTHERS

AT one time the Howrigan brothers were the biggest Maple producers in Franklin County, Vermont. Of Irish heritage, whose families settled in Vermont in the early 1800s, the dairy farming brothers were very successful farmers who produced excellent Maple syrup. While visiting with Bob Howrigan, I asked how much syrup they cumulatively produced. He told me he did not know. I was surprised because they were a very close Irish family. "No," he said, "I want to show you something." He took me to his shed where stacks of thirty-five-gallon Maple barrels were stored. "See those barrels?" he said, "I sometimes fill them with water, so my brothers are fooled when they come around. They kick them to see which ones are full."

Senator Aiken

NOT TRUSTING A NEW PRESIDENT

GEORGE Aiken and President Truman served together as U.S. Senators. I was having lunch with Lola Aiken, the Senator's wife, and she told me an intriguing story about Truman and Aiken. Truman became president when Roosevelt died in Warm Springs, Arkansas. Shortly after his swearing in, he called Aiken and asked, "George, do you know anyone in the war department who can tell me what is going on, for these bastards won't tell me anything." Aiken had a friend, a Colonel Gibson from Vermont who served in the intelligence unit in the war department. He told Truman he would get him over to brief the President. Aiken forgot, and a couple of days later, Truman called again and said, "George, where the hell is your friend?" Finally, Aiken arranged for his colonel friend (later he would be Judge Gibson) to visit the president. According to Lola, the war department did not yet trust the new president and was not telling him about the atomic bomb.

DON'T RAISE MY RETIREMENT!

WHILE serving as Vermont commissioner of agriculture (secretary), I annually held the Aiken Awards to recognize contributions to agriculture. The governor, ex-governors, and Senator Aiken's widow were invitees. Lola, the widow of the senator, and I became good friends. She presented me with a signed copy of Aiken's Senate diary. Lola became his chief of staff and was a masterful administrator and people person. She died in September 5, 2014, and her memory led me back to the diary. In his last entry on January 2, 1975, he wrote about his retirement pay: "I could have added 7.5% by resigning before midnight on December 31st. I did not choose to do so, because I have always felt I should carry out contracts in full. When I came to Washington, I lost a week in the Senate because I insisted on completing my term as governor of Vermont. I have never been sorry I did this."

HE WAS A SKINNY LITTLE KID!

MY grandmother graduated from Brattleboro High School in Brattleboro, Vermont in 1909 with Senator George Aiken. It was a small school with a small class. She and Aiken corresponded every year about the time of the class reunion. In high school, my grandmother was an attractive and talented young lady. I loved teasing her, and one time, asked her if Senator Aiken ever kissed her behind an old wagon. "No," she said, "he was just a skinny little kid!"

DECLARE VICTORY AND GET THE HELL OUT!

AMBASSADOR Bunker lived in Dummerston, Vermont. He served as ambassador to Vietnam when I was serving in Vietnam on the U.S.S. *America*. I often wondered how an intelligent man could work under such conditions. He was a personal friend of George Aiken, our U.S. Senator from Putney, Vermont. I guess his advice did get through to his friend, for it was Aiken who advised Nixon to declare victory and get the hell out of Vietnam. My childhood friend from Dummerston was serving in combat in Vietnam. He wrote a letter to Bunker telling him he was a Dummerston neighbor and in constant combat where his life was constantly threatened. Bunker wrote him back and said he looked forward to seeing him when he returned to Dummerston!

JUST SAY A PRAYER

AT one time, it was not unusual for U.S. Senators from opposite parties to become friends. Senator Aiken started having breakfast every day with Senator Mike Mansfield, a Midwest Democrat. When Senator Aiken died, the family carried out his wishes and held a small service. A friend of the family was helping with the telephone calls and received a call from the Kennedy family requesting attendance at the service. He politely told them it was a small family service, and they could pray for the Senator. The Kennedy's sent flowers and had their friend, Cardinal Cushing of Boston, conduct a mass for Senator Aiken.

WOOD LOOKS LIKE WOOD

RAY was a rugged Vermonter who lived in Athens, Vermont. He was dirt poor and would give you the shirt off his back if you were in need. He and his family of four lived in an old brick schoolhouse hardly big enough for two people. It was situated along the dirt road as you passed through Athens on your way to Cambridgeport, Vermont. Ray was often hired to help in the Allbee sawmill where he tirelessly rolled the logs onto the carriage and tailed the saw where the boards came flying off the cut log. Ray was of Irish/English ancestry and looked like a strong Englishman who spent hours in the pub. He liked his beer but was never abusive of his drinking during work. He always had a funny story or yarn to tell, and his humor was infectious. The mill workers in the 1950s did not earn much money—slightly more than the owners of the mill who often did not take home a paycheck. Too augment his income Ray would cut cord wood to sell to neighbors and others in the valley. The wood was piled near his house so he could keep good watch over the resource. One weekend, he took his family to visit relatives. He came home and discovered a substantial amount of his dried cord wood was missing. In a small town, it did not take long to learn who took the wood. Ray discovered his wood was stolen by some out-of-state hunters who owned a cabin a mile or so from his house. Ray called the state police who told him "wood looks like wood," and they could not prove it was his wood. Had the camp owners asked Ray for some wood he probably would have given it to them or at least exchanged it for some beer. He cut more wood and marked a piece with a special treatment. He drilled a hole in a piece and inserted a half stick of dynamite. It was then quite easy to buy dynamite for construction projects. He covered the dynamite and hole with some sawdust and glue so one would not notice the intrusion in the wood. He took his family on another trip and more of his wood had disappeared. It wasn't long before an explosion at the cabin blew off half the chimney. Fortunately, no one was in the cabin at the time. The police were called to investigate, and they could not determine where the wood came from, as wood looks like wood!

HOW TO FIND A RABBIT DOG

JULES, my hunting and fishing buddy, spent much of his youth in Northfield, Vermont with an uncle who owned a meat market. Jules talked about his love of rabbit hunting and how he would find rabbit dogs. He would drive around Northfield with a good bone and entice a local beagle in his car. He would then spend the day hunting with the dog and return it back to the pickup location.

I WILL BURY YOU!

EVERETT, a mentally disabled man from Grafton, Vermont performed odd jobs and generally made himself known in the community by visiting everyone. He was harmless, and it was evident he was mentally handicapped. I was painting the interior of the refinished Grafton Foundation Houses as a summer job, and Everett would often stop by to say hello. My boss would often tease poor Everett as would other people in town. Whenever Everett showed up, my boss would say "Everett, Ron is your father." Everett would get quite upset and tell him he knew who his father was and I, Ron, was not his father. This went on for some time whenever Everett showed up at the work site. One day, Everett said, "You may make fun of me, but I dig the holes you are buried in." Everett dug the cemetery graves for extra money and always had the last laugh.

THOUGHT THE LIQUOR WOULD FREEZE

RAYMOND was a painting and caretaking contractor who ran a crew maintaining houses in the West River Valley. My twin brother worked for Raymond. John Kenneth Galbraith, a world-famous economist, who served as Kennedy's Ambassador to India, maintained a summer home in Townshend, Vermont. Raymond was the caretaker of the house and was always painting and maintaining the place. My twin brother had an insider's view of history during the summer of 1965 as people came and went, and Galbraith was receiving calls from President Johnson. Raymond would close the house up in the late fall. In the spring he opened the house up. One spring when Galbraith came back, he asked Raymond, "Where did my liquor go?" Without hesitation, Raymond replied, "Professor Galbraith, I took it because I thought it would freeze!"

I WILL NOT WAKE HIM DURING HIS NAP

WHEN Roger was working for Raymond painting the inside of Professor Galbraith's house in the 1960s, he would often hear Emily, the housekeeper, answer the phone and tell the Professor it was President Johnson on the line. Many years later, the professor's son Peter told Roger a funny story about Emily answering the phone. Dr. Galbraith was taking a nap when the president's secretary called and asked to speak to the economist. Emily told the person he was taking a nap and she did not wake him from his naps. Very shortly thereafter, the president called and asked to speak to Galbraith. Emily informed the president he was taking a nap and she was not about to wake him from his nap. When Galbraith woke up, Emily told him about the call from Johnson. Galbraith called the president and started to apologize for his housekeeper. Johnson told him not to apologize for he needed a person like Emily and wanted to hire her!

DIFFICULT DOCTOR

DURING the summer of my college years I worked for a local painting contractor. Oscar was one of the painters I worked with that summer. He was a World War II veteran and saw seventeen months of service in a submarine at sea without seeing land in the South Pacific. He told stories of siphoning torpedo juice through bread and drinking it. He saw much action at sea, and when he got home, he just drank. Were it not for his wife, he would have stayed drunk. Oscar was one of those rare individuals with an exceptional IQ who read, painted, was a master cabinet maker, and could discuss any subject. In addition, he was a master interior house painter and taught me much about painting. One day, our boss told us we would be painting the interior of a house for a retired heart surgeon. He said the heart surgeon was difficult to please, and we would probably not see our boss very often because of he wished to avoid the surgeon. We should not expect him to rescue us from the difficult doctor. The doctor watched over us with a hawk's eye the first day. Every move was watched to ensure we knew what we were doing and were not dripping paint on his floor or window sashes. The doctor's success in life was evident, for he had carbon copies of hearts throughout his study and many books on the shelf bore his name. During the first day, Oscar started talking to him about hearts, health, and various other subjects. The doctor knew a kindred spirit in intelligence and professionalism when he saw one, and he and Oscar became fast friends. By the third day, he was inviting us to lunch, serving us tea, and looking out for our overall welfare. We started enjoying our work for the doctor. Whenever our boss asked about the job, we told him it would be better if he stayed away due to the very difficult doctor!

Al Foley

⬦⬦⬦⬦⬦⬦

AL Foley served as a representative from Norwich, Vermont in the early 1970s. He was a retired emeritus professor of history at Dartmouth and was also a collector and publisher of Vermont stories. Al was often bored upstairs during the sessions and would come down to my office to tell me stories. He published many of his stories in a book. He knew I was from a small Vermont town and would enjoy his Vermont humor and stories. The following are some of Al's stories as told to me. A variation is in his book.

DON'T DUMP THE ENTIRE LOAD!

A substitute minister was giving his first sermon in a small Vermont church. There was a very small congregation that Sunday. The minister delivered his long and his fire and brimstone sermon. After the sermon, he asked one of the parishioners, who happened to be a farmer, what he thought of the sermon. The farmer replied, "Reverend, I am a farmer, and I keep some heifers in one of my pastures. Every week, I take a load of hay up to the heifers. Sometimes, there are a few heifers, and sometimes, the entire herd is assembled. If there are only a few heifers, I don't dump the entire load!"

MOTION FOR ANOTHER PREGNANCY

PRIOR to the sexual and cultural revolution of the 1960s and 1970s, bearing a child out of wedlock was socially unacceptable. Often, if the young woman failed to seek wedlock with the father of the child, she was sent to the Lund Home in Burlington where the child was born and put up for adoption. The state would pay for the cost of the home and reimburse towns for the initial expense. Town meetings are an important part of Vermont's history, and voters are free to ask questions about budgets and various issues relating to town business. One of the voters, when looking over the budget, noticed the town paid to send a young lady to the Burlington Lund home. He also noticed the town was reimbursed by the state. He said, "Mr. Moderator, is it true the town spent $100 to pay for Miss A's trip to the Lund home?" The moderator answered, "Yes, that was the expense." "Well," said the voter, "is it true the town was reimbursed $200 by the State?" "Yes," answered the moderator. "Mr. Moderator, if my calculations are correct, the town made $100." "Yes," answered the Moderator. "Well, Mr. Moderator, I move we get her pregnant again!"

SUPPORTING CONSTITUENTS

VERMONT had not enacted a doe season for deer. It was a divisive issue, for historically only bucks were hunted and does were allowed to winter over. The fish and game department proposed a doe season requiring legislative approval. Legislators returned to their hometowns for the town meetings. At the meetings, they would brief the assembled on the issues of the day and take questions from the voters. One legislator returned to his town with the knowledge he would be asked several questions on his position on the proposed doe season. As he stood before the assembly, a voter asked, "What is your position on the proposed doe season?" The legislator looked at the assembly and said, "I know each of you. I have prayed with you, played with you, and watched your children grow. I know some of you support doe season, and some of you are opposed. I want you to know I support your positions."[1]

FLAPPER AND DAMN GOOD ONE

GERI was my 100-year-old friend who owned the Post Office building in Essex, New York. She was an entrepreneurial woman who owned two movie theatres in the area in the fifties and sixties. She always dressed in style and kept abreast of the latest developments. I once asked her what the 1920s were like, since she was born in 1906 and in 1926 was a mere 20 years old. She said she was a "Flapper and a damned good one."

THIS IS NOT HEAVEN!

GERI, my 95-year-old Essex, New York friend, was in the Plattsburg, New York hospital for a procedure. She was about to have an operation for an embolism, and the doctor asked me to discuss a DNR (do not

---

1   Allen R Foley, *What The Old Timer Said* (Vermont, Stephen Green Press, 1971)

resuscitate) with her. He wanted her to sign the DNR should anything unusual occur during the operation. I explained the DNR was the same she had signed and placed on her refrigerator in her residence. I said the hospital needed a new DNR for her operation. She turned to me and said, "Tear that paper up!" So, I did as she said and told the doctor she was not signing the paper. They went ahead with the operation, and as she was recovering, I entered the recovery room. She opened her eyes and said, "This is not heaven, this is not where I am supposed to be!"

VERMONT, THE WELCOMING COUNTRY

DURING the 1970s the Killington ski area in Sherburne, Vermont tested the idea of using sewage effluent water in snowmaking. Unfortunately, the press got hold of it, and it became a front-page news item: "Where the Effluent Meets the Affluent." The ski area decided to forgo the idea.

Al Moulton, a friend who served on many occasions as the economic development secretary or commissioner, coined the term "Vermont, the beckoning country." On another occasion, Vermont tested another term "Vermont, the ski capital, a lot goes on when the skis come off!" Due to pressure, they never used the second term.

SPANISH PARTRIDGE

MY wife's uncle was my hunting and fishing buddy. Jules was a Spanish boy who grew up in Northfield, Vermont. He served honorably during World War II serving as a tail gunner in a B29 in Europe. He then used the GI Bill to acquire a degree in business from the University of Vermont. He worked as a buyer for IBM. Jules loved to hunt and fish, and we would often go partridge hunting. Partridge, and or ruffled grouse, is a weary bird and difficult to shoot. We would often come up empty-handed because neither of us were great shots. However, when we were out hunting, he always shot a blue jay for his polenta, a Spanish dish of boiled cornmeal. I always referred to blue jays as Spanish partridges.!

BEING SPIED ON

DR. Otis, our family doctor in Townshend, Vermont, was invited to the Soviet Union with other U.S. physicians in the early 1960s. It was the time of the Cold War when the two countries were hostile toward each other. On his return he told about staying in a hotel with the other doctors. They all assumed their actions were being watched and their conversations were being recorded. Such was the fear permeating all contacts between the two countries. The doctors were in a conference room and noticed a wire running up the wall. They thought the wire was part of a recording device hidden in the ceiling. One of the doctors took out a tweezer and snapped the wire. When he did , the chandelier in the conference room fell to the floor!

HIGGINS'S STORE AND POST OFFICE

MR. Higgins ran the Newfane general store which also served as the post office. The activity occurred around four in the afternoon when the mail truck arrived from Brattleboro with the mail and newspapers. Otherwise, the store did not carry much and had seen its peak in a bygone era with horses and wagons. The hitching posts still stood outside the store. One time, someone asked Mr. Higgins for a product, and he said he did not carry it for "it sold too fast."

MAKING HIS OWN CASKET

WHEN my son was a student at the University of Vermont, I suggested we take a drive one spring day and visit sugarhouses. We drove to Fairfield, Vermont where dairy friends operated large sugaring operations. We stopped at Francis sugarhouse. His son and daughter-in-law were boiling. I asked for Francis, and they told me they could not tell me where he was. I introduced myself and they recognized me and said he was in the barn making his own casket. They suggested I go and talk to him . I thanked them and said I would let him continue privately making his casket. Two years later Francis died; he was laid out in his living room in his handmade casket from the hardwood on his farm.

HOW TO FIX A BRIDGE

FRANCIS served as road commissioner for the town of Fairfield. He provided equipment and labor, often without a charge. A bridge beam over a river was cracked after a truck with too much weight tried to navigate the bridge. The state highway agency looked at the bridge and told Francis a new expensive bridge was required. The proposed bridge would cost the town thousands of dollars. Francis told them he would wait and see what would happen in the winter. When winter came and ice froze the pool below the bridge, Francis went to work. He jacked up the bridge and replaced the beam. The bridge was repaired at a small fraction of the cost of a new bridge. Such was the ingenuity of a Vermont Yankee.

WHO WILL DIE FIRST?

TED, our Brookline neighbor, suffered the loss of his first wife. Roger and I were asked to be pallbearers at her funeral. Shortly after her death Ted met another woman. She thought he had money and he thought she was well off. Roger and I did not view it as a marriage made in heaven. We often visited with Ted, and one day we knocked on the door and asked to see Ted. She told us "poor Ted" was tired and we should return the next day. We started walking out of the yard when we heard her yelling at Ted to "Get his fat ass out of bed and start doing some work around the house." She was trying to kill him by overworking him. Unfortunately, she died suddenly of cancer and there was little money left for Ted.

THE FREEMEN

THE Army Corps of Engineers proposed building a large dam in the West River Valley in the 1940s. The dam would be located in Dummerston and flood much of the West River Valley, creating a very large lake. Many towns in the valley would be flooded by the proposed dam. The residents of the valley rose up in opposition and formed a vigilante group opposed to the location and construction of the dam. The picture below shows members armed with their guns, including our family doctor and many leaders in the valley community. Eventually, the Corps of Engineers compromised and built two dams, one in West Townshend and the other in

Jamaica, Vermont. Both dams, while not destroying the towns, changed the ecological balance of the river. Brown trout no longer swam up the river to spawn and the ice flows which cleaned the riverbeds and banks ceased.

DR. LEACH AND PRESIDENT HOOVER

DURING the summer we worked mowing lawns and performing other yard services for retired people. I worked for a retired engineer and Roger worked for a retired doctor. The doctor was a humanitarian and served with the American Red Cross and was interred by the Japanese during World War II. He loved gardening and would work alongside Roger in his garden. One day, he was called to the telephone, and when he returned, he told Roger he had just spoken to a former Stanford roommate. He said, "Roger, that was President Hoover. He and I were roommates at Stanford. I know history is not treating him well. However, I want you to remember he is a great man!" He was close to President Hoover and participated in some of the greatest health care emergencies of the twentieth century. His name is inscribed in three separate places in the Hoover Tow.

CHAPTER 4

ANIMALS

YOU learn many things from animals. You about a person by how he or she treats animals. Our farm was full of animals. My first memory was of the workhorses and sugaring as we gathered sap and the horses dragged the sled. Of course, there were cows and calves, pigs, chickens, geese, cats, dogs, deer, woodchucks, squirrels, beavers, birds, and assorted other animals around the farm. Some animals were used to feed our family, and some were either pets or work animals. We treated all the animals well and honored those the fed our families.

SPINNING A DOG WHO CHASED DEER IN A BARREL

HERMAN was a beagle dog my father acquired as a puppy hoping he would grow into a good rabbit hound. We took him out rabbit hunting and he chased two good-sized rabbits. They were taller than rabbits, ran faster, and had big white tails. In fact, they looked like deer! My father decided Herman needed a treatment to avoid deer. He asked the game warden who said to feed Herman a good meal, wipe him all over with deer carrion, and roll him in an old oil barrel with an attached lid. We were in high school and thought the Herman treatment would be good for other dogs, and we would have a business treating dogs who were guilty of chasing deer. We fed Herman his favorite meal. We then spread the dead deer carrion over his body. Finally, we put him in the barrel and locked the door. We then rolled the barrel up hills, down hills, and through the fields until we were tired. We opened the barrel door and Herman reluctantly came out. He came out wagging his tail and immediately went into the barrel waiting for another ride. Instead of the desired reaction, he loved the meal, the smell was tolerable, and the ride was just the best thing he had experienced in a long time. So, Herman dashed our business hopes and continued chasing deer.

GETTING A COW OUT OF A WELL/DIRTY WATER

HE was a well-known and respected Connecticut medical doctor who purchased a Brookline hill dairy farm. His wife, while accomplished, did not fit in well with the small community. A dairy cow fell into the well and men in the community were called to help rescue the cow. They assessed the situation as they looked at the floundering animal in the well. They built a tripod over the well and attached a pulley. One of the men was dropped into the well so he could attach a rope around the animal. The end of the rope was attached to a work horse, and on command, the horse pulled the frightened cow out of the well . The cow as none the worse for wear, but a little lighter due to what was left behind. The cow emptied her intestines into the well, and the water became smelly and brown. The men poured some Clorox into the well and secured the top. Due to their lack of fondness for the woman of the house, they did not to tell her about the well and cow. When she drew the water. she would say it was of a brownish color and smelled. All who knew of the animal in the well would smile silently.

WAS HE A MAD DOG?

MY twin brother and I were close, but we were often fighting to see who was stronger and faster. Our fighting would upset our dog Herman and he would try to break it up by pulling on our clothing or biting us. One time, I was without shoes, and Herman managed to bite through my foot. The foot became infected and required treatment. I was a freshman at UVM. When I returned to school, I went to the infirmary for continued treatment. The nurse looked at the foot and asked me what happened? I told her a dog had bitten my foot and caused the infection. She asked if it was a mad dog? I said the dog that bit me was not a happy dog!

PET GREY SQUIRRIL

WE were partridge hunting with my father on a rainy late September day when we found two baby squirrels lying in the leaves. From their size, we assumed they were no more than a day old and they were abandoned. We took them home, warmed them up, and started feeding them milk with a medicine dropper. One of the babies died. The other squirrel thrived and bonded to us as though we were his parents. The squirrel ran around our house like a pet cat, except it would chew wooden furniture. When male friends came to the house, the squirrel ran up one leg of their pants and down the other leg. Of course, it was uncomfortable when the squirrel reached the half- way point. When we took the squirrel outside, it would follow us like a cat until it heard a noise, and then it would run back to the house. I loved watching the squirrel ride on my father's shoulder as he went to feed the pigs. That little pet gave me a new appreciation for squirrels and their intelligence. Unfortunately, the little pet squirrel died one morning from distemper.

SQUIRRELS ARE CATHOLICS

MY wife and I owned a long-legged Jack Russel Terrier who was fast and loved to chase squirrels. We lived near the Catholic Center at the University of Vermont. I took the dog on a walk near the center where he caught and killed a squirrel. He took the dead animal up next to the steps of the Catholic Center, dug a hole, and buried the animal. I then learned squirrels were Catholics, and the dog was trying to place the animal as close to the church as possible.

RACOON WITH A HEADACHE

THERE was no store in Brookline, so whenever we needed an item we went "over street" to Newfane. One day, we were returning from "over street," and a very large raccoon ran in front of the car. My father could not avoid the animal, and we heard a large thump as the car and the raccoon connected. My father stopped the car and picked up the withering raccoon by the tail. Believing the coon was in his death throes, my father swung the animal over his head and slammed its head down on the road for a humane kill. He threw the animal into the trunk of the car. We arrived home and lifted the trunk and the animal was alive. We took the raccoon and placed it in the empty chicken house, figuring it would either die or live and we would find out in the morning. We opened the chicken house door the following morning and the raccoon quickly emerged. He took one look around, took his bearings, and headed back in the direction of Newfane. What a headache he must have suffered!

HORSE SENSE

MY father and uncle owned two workhorses named Nellie and Chub. Nellie was rust colored with a beautiful golden mane and Chub was black. Nellie was the team leader with a strong personality. They were normally housed in the farm barn in a stall adjacent to the cattle. They were used in the woods to haul logs to the skid ways and to gather sap during sugaring season. Skid ways were ramps made from logs to roll cut logs onto carriages. My father hired a worker to cut timber on a timber lot 3 miles from the farm. Nellie and Chub were housed at the site in a lean two made from lumber mill slabs. When the logger was finished logging for the day he fed and watered the horses and put them in the lean too for the next day's work. The local logger was paid by the hour for an 8-hour day. Unfortunately, he liked his beer and started drinking early and worked less than 8 hours. Other than measuring the timber cut daily one would not know less than 8 hours was worked. His undoing was not properly caring for the horses. When he finished the early and unhooked the horses, Chub was very obedient and went into the lean. Nellie had a mind of her own and knew the direction and location of her real home. When she was unhooked, she took off for the farm and ran by the mill about 2:30 or 3:00 p.m. Nellie gave the logger away. My father started paying the logger by the board feet of logs cut rather than by the hour. A horse called "Nellie" gave the logger away.

SALTY PICKLES

BILL was like another older brother or another son to my parents. He was a single bachelor who was a friend of the family and lived a few houses up the road. He often visited and sometimes often ate dinner with us. One evening he brought along his mother's pet bulldog he was watching. My parents decided to take a picnic at the public picnic area on Putney Mountain with a nice viewing area. Everyone, including the dog, piled into the car. My father drove us up the winding curves of the mountain until we arrived at the parking area. Someone had laid a blanket on the nearby grass with all their food laid out as though they were going to eat. They left it as they walked out to the overlook, some 200 yards from the parking area. We opened the car door and the dog quickly jumped out and headed straight for the picnic on the blanket. We tried to catch the dog, but he reached the blanket first and raised his leg over the open pickle jar and emptied his bladder directly into the jar. We were horrified and did not know what to do. We gathered the dog before he could do any more damage to the picnic and placed him into the car. My parents decided with the dog a picnic on the ground was not possible, and we drove home. We had our picnic at our home. I always wondered if the dog's actions affected the taste of the pickles.

CHAPTER 5

YOUTH

WE spent our youth in the West River Valley in the small towns of Brookline, Newfane, and Townshend. Brattleboro was our shopping and cultural center where my parents shopped once a week. The area supplied much of our education beyond the two-room school in Brookline and the high school in Townshend. The West River flowed through the valley and supplied many recreational activities in the summer months. The woods were full of wildlife, and it was not unusual to see sixty to seventy deer feeding in a field in early spring. The news was carried by person, the local newspaper, or by radio and later television. Local news was also communicated at the local stores and the town dump. Phone calls were made from home or from pay phone booths. It was both the best of times and the worst of times. We had little, but we had an abundance of friends, family, and a warm and caring environment.

SOAP IN THE MOUTH

MY father and uncle employed seven men in the lumber mill. Our home was 300 yards from the mill. When we were about five years of age, we would walk down to the mill and watch the men work. When the mill was shut down to file the saws, we would venture into the mill and listen to the men share stories. The language employed was often cultural and basic. We learned many new words and some words we had heard in church. We tried some of the new words on my mother. We were so excited and started with some of words we had heard in church. She told us never to use those words again in her presence and shoved soap into our mouths. We really could not understand, since we had heard the minister use Jesus Christ and God in church!

HAMMERING SAWS

THE first time my father took us to Walpole, New Hampshire to have the mill saws hammered, we did not know what he was talking about. The saws were five feet in diameter, and we could not imagine why anyone would hammer a saw.. We learned it was like tuning a piano. The older gentleman was proficient in hammering and placed the saw in a horizontal position and started hammering it in different areas while listening to the sound it produced. He was balancing the saw by hammering it in different places. He would watch it and hear the sound to determine if it was properly balanced. A saw not properly balanced would not cut properly and would wobble as it cut thru the log.

READING PAPER FLOATING ON BACK

THE West River was our bathtub away from home in the summer. We swam, fished, and bathed in the river. There was a small beach on the river on the Brookline side of the bridge. It was prior to the construction of the Townshend Dam and the dam beach. People from around the area swam at the Brookline beach. We took our Red Cross swimming lessons on the beach every summer, forcing ourselves to climb into the water often less than sixty degrees. Sometimes, we would take my Aunt Gladys and her daughter to the swimming beach. Gladys was a wonderful woman who lived with my grandfather and took care of his needs. Unfortunately, she inherited the fat gene from one side of the family. I fondly remember her floating in the West River and reading the newspaper… she floated so well not a piece of the paper took on any water.

NEAR DEATH IN A ROAD SANDER

IT was a cold and slippery winter night, and the roads had to be sanded to prevent vehicles from sliding on the ice. The sand pit was adjacent to our house, and my father and uncle were charged with plowing and sanding all the Brookline roads. It was a duty they took seriously, and I have fond memories of riding with my father in an Old-World War II army truck with a dump body plowing and sanding the roads. I always marveled at his ability to work until two in the morning plowing the roads in a truck with no heat, windshield wipers that hardly worked, and a constant noise. Henry Bush and I were selected to ride on the sander attached to the body of the truck. The sander had one wheel that caused the sand to spread out along the road. However, to operate effectively, two people had to stand with one foot on the sander and one foot on the truck body and shovel the sand into the sander as the truck body was tipped to a forty-five-degree angle. The only connection that solidified the sander to the truck body were two old hooks and check chains. Otherwise, the sander would disconnect from the body, and the two people would be thrown with the sand between the truck body and the sander, acting like a quickly closing knife to cut the two bodies in half. My father was normally safety conscious and always checked the chains. He was a person who worked with saws all his life and never lost a finger or other body part. Somehow, on this particular night, he forgot. Henry and I were busy shoveling sand when our world fell apart. The sander was not properly hooked, and it came free from the truck body. We and the sand quickly fell between the truck body and the sander before it again came back against the truck body like a large knife. Henry and I woke up on the ground amongst the sand. We realized we just missed being cut in half by no more than one second. It was the night they almost buried both of us in a pile of sand. I can't think of a better person to have left the earth with than Henry Bush.

GIVE ME YOUR LIQUOR

HORSE pulling was an annual event at the New Brook Field Days. My father and uncle supplied the equipment to operate the pulling contest. Many of the pulling groups were loggers, and it was a group who naturally loved their liquor and good times. My good friend whose father was a gunsmith brought a pistol loaded with caps to the Field Days. We were showing it to some of the pullers when one asked to borrow it for a few minutes. He was kind, but rather a rough-looking man. He walked over to some of the other pullers and pointed the pistol at them and told them to hand over their booze. They could not believe what was happening and did as they were told. When they handed over the booze, he pulled the trigger to shoot one of them. The gun went off, and nothing happened. They realized they were being fooled and had some fun roughing him up a little. But it all ended with them drinking together and joking.

BONDO AND RIVET GUNS

WE did not purchase a new car every year. My father was handy with a rivet gun and bondo, which often held our cars and trucks together. In the 1950s and 1960s, automobiles and trucks suffered greatly from the salt placed on the highways in the winter months. My wife's father was a manager for General Motors and as part of his employment he received a new Cadillac every year. I tell people the difference between our fathers was my father received a new can of bondo and pop rivets every year, while her father received a new car!

SHUT UP, KID, AND GET ON THE LIFT

ALTHOUGH I grew up skiing, most of my early skiing was on a rope tow and a T-bar. It was not until my high school years I finally had the opportunity to sit on an actual chair lift. Killington was a new ski area, and we were attending a high school ski meet. There was a sign next to the lift advising those who had never used a chair to ask the attendant for assistance. I skied up to the chair and informed the attendant of my lack of experience. He said, "Shut up, kid, and get on the chair."

CATCHING A BEAVER WHILE FISHING

GRASSY Brooke flows through the center of Brookline and once contained many beaver dams. The dams were a wonderful place to catch trout. I waded through the water to the edge of the beaver dam with my fishing pole and bait. The water was clear as I threw my line to the center of the stream. In the corner of my eyes, I saw a beaver swimming under the water toward my line in the water. As I started lifting my line out of the water, the beaver swam by, and my hook connected with his coat. I pulled on the line with the hope that my hook would break free, but it was evident that he or she was well hooked. As I pulled on the hook and line, the beaver felt the pressure. It did not take the beaver long before it turned its head toward the line and bit through it with its sharp teeth. Suddenly, my line was free without its hook and bait or beaver.

PAINTING TED CORBETT'S HOUSE

OUR neighbor Ted Corbett purchased the house up the road from our home. Ted was a retired insurance man from New York City. He was a small and wiry Irishman who grew up in the city, the son of Irish immigrants. Ted traveled in his youth to California where he appeared as an extra in some Charlie Chaplin movies. Ted also fought as a bantamweight boxer. During our college years, Ted asked us to paint his house with the understanding he would pay us with excess furniture and other goods. Since we really liked Ted, we agreed to the arrangement. Ted told us he would buy the paint, red barn paint, which if applied properly was not to be thinned with paint thinner. We advised Ted his house would take at least six gallons of red and two gallons of white. Ted came home with two gallons of red, four gallons of paint thinner, and one gallon of white paint. We thinned the red paint and applied it like water. Amazingly, the house did not look bad even though the paint was too thin.

WALKING BETWEEN SAWS IN THE LUMBER MILL

LUMBER mills and saws are dangerous. Knots can break free from a log and fly through a mill, or someone can fall and injure himself or herself on a saw. As children, we would often run between a working saw and the log carriage, not thinking of the deadly injury we would incur if we fell. We would jump around the log piles unaware that at any time one of the logs could roll onto us. We were too young to worry about the danger and obviously felt we were fast on our feet.

BURYING A DOLL/BIRTHDAY

HERBERT (Doug) was our best friend and neighbor in Brookline. When he was five, he asked for and received a doll for his birthday. He loved the doll, but Roger and I, being less than understanding at that age, teased him unceremoniously over his doll. Now, I can only imagine what we said to him and how it hurt him. Our teasing was so constant he took the doll out and buried it in his yard. When Doug turned fifty, I sent him a new doll with a note attached saying I was sorry for our actions.

DO YOU HAVE PRINCE ALBERT IN A CAN?

GRACE and Dellard ran the small filling station in Newfane where my father would gas up his vehicles. Grace was really the operator as Dellard worked out in the woods cutting logs. Prince Albert was a type of tobacco product sold in a can with the Prince's picture. As youths, we would call the station and ask if they had Prince Albert in the can. When Grace said they did, we would say, "Then let him out!" I am sure she grew tired of that prank, but she never let on.

I CAN BOIL FASTER THAN YOU CAN GATHER!

SUGARING season was our favorite time of year. My family hung approximately 2,200 buckets we gathered with a sled pulled behind a bulldozer. I have fond memories of hiking in deep snow, spilling buckets of sap on my pants, and riding the sled back to the sugarhouse. My grandfather boiled the sap until he died in 1962. After his death, my uncle started boiling. He was always telling those of us who gathered he could boil faster than we could gather the sap. One day, we decided we had enough of his boasting. On our next gathering trip, we stopped at the brook and filled up the gathering tank and returned to the sugar house. We emptied that water in the holding tank and returned to the woods to gather some more sap. When we returned with the next load, he was boiling away wondering why he was not producing as much syrup and not keeping up with our gathering. He never boasted about not keeping up again!

KIDS SHOULD NOT SHOOT AT OTHER KIDS WITH LOADED GUNS

WHEN we were about ten, our close neighbors, the Howe's, moved to Brattleboro and rented out their house. The occupants of the house were a Vermont game warden, his wife, and his ten-year-old son. The first thing we noticed was their unfriendliness and a young boy who had difficulty relating to other children. We were a pretty friendly group of kids, but we did not take kindly to pugnacious kids. Somehow, my cousin Neal, Roger, and I started arguing with the son. I'm not sure what the argument was about, but the kid suddenly became very angry and ran into his house. We stood there uncertain what was happening when he started shooting at us from inside the house with a .22 rifle. Fortunately, none of the shots hit us as we dived behind a log. He kept shooting, and the bullets were flying over our heads. We kept yelling at him to stop the shooting. Finally, he ran out of bullets. We yelled at him to drop the gun and come out of the house. He did as he was told, and we admonished him for using a gun against us or any other person. Our parents taught us gun safety, and we were surprised his father, a game warden, had not provided the same instruction. He pleaded with us not to tell either his or our parents about what happened. We told him if he promised never to do so again, we would not tell anyone. We did not tell our parents, and I suspect when his father found the ammunition missing the son admitted his action. Shortly after the shooting, the game warden and his family packed up their belongings and moved away.

THE SOVIETS ARE AHEAD!

SPUTNIK was a total surprise to our government when it was launched in 1957. I remember going to the store with my father when he bought *The Brattleboro Reformer* with the Sputnik headline. Our country was convinced the Soviets with its launching were ahead of us in technology and education. Many a night, we would stand in our yard in Brookline and watch Sputnik blink over the sky. Fortunately, the threat propelled scientific education in America.

CHIPMUNK CROSSING

THERE was little traffic by our house in the 50's, as there were not many people in town… population of 104. Chipmunks are small rodents and were quite plentiful. It was not uncommon to see them skirt across the road in front of you when you were in a car or riding your bicycle. Sometimes, their dash would fail, and they were visibly squashed in the road. We thought we would have fun and made a sign for the highway that said, "Caution Chipmunk Crossing."

HIT THEM HARDER.

BOBBY and Doug were our best friends and neighbors. We were always playing together. Sides would change. Sometimes, one of us would team up with one of them and vice versa. One day, it was us two Albee's against the two Howes in a stone-throwing battle. The battle did not last long as Luna, their mother, broke up the fight and told Bobby and Doug their father would punish them when he came home. It was not long before Robert drove into the yard and received the report from Luna. We dove into the woods across from their house to watch the punishment. Robert told them to pull down their pants. They did as they were told, and he took off his belt and gave them several lashes across their bottoms. I don't think they were strong lashes for Robert was a kind and thoughtful man who loved his children. However, for us who never received any punishment from our father, it was a surprise. Although Roger and I felt sorry for them, we were also encouraging Robert to hit them harder so they would not throw any more stones.

IS IT A COLLAPSIBLE CANOE?

IN the summer, the swimming hole under the bridge that connected Newfane and Brookline was our recreational area and our bathtub. Canoeists were often floating by us as we were swimming. Roger and I wanted a canoe but did not have enough money for a purchase. We found an advertisement in the *Field and Stream* magazine for a canoe kit for less than $50.00. Receiving it after purchasing, we found it came in a box with a few small cedar strips, small tacks, and a large piece of canvas. The directions were quite simple… make a frame from the cedar strips and attach the canvas with the tacks. Then paint the canvas with waterproof epoxy paint. We painted the canoe an ugly green, and it looked like one half of a poorly constructed bathtub. We were not sure of its ability to float comfortably in the water or hold us… surely, it would leak, or the cedar strips would break. We launched it in the West River and were successfully paddling through a swimming hole. While it did not look fancy or like a canoe, we congratulated ourselves on our accomplishment. Certainly, it would serve our purposes. A woman swimmer looked at us and yelled, "Is that a collapsible canoe?" We told her we hoped it wasn't. At a beach party on the West River at the end of the summer, we started a fire in the canoe and watched it as it floated down the river burning.

GAS ENGINES DON'T RUN ON FUEL OIL!

MY father and uncle maintained two fuel pumps, one for gasoline and the other for diesel fuel. Since we often worked in the mill or on the road for free, we often filled up our pickup at the pump. We knew by custom which pump was fuel oil and which was gasoline… we needn't smell. One day, we were in a hurry for school and stopped and quickly pumped some fuel into the truck. Little did we realize they changed the pumps and we pumped diesel fuel into a gasoline truck. We did not drive very far when smoke started coming out the back of the pickup, and it just stopped. We left it beside the road, and my father drained the tank and put the correct fuel in so we could drive it again.

THOSE CRAFTY BEAVERS

BEAVERS are ingenious little animals. They build dams which make the army corps of engineers look like amateurs. There is nothing more enjoyable than visiting a beaver dam and watching the beautiful animals go about their activities. Unfortunately, dams are sometimes built in places obstructing highways and culverts. Grassy Brook runs the entire length of Brookline, and it was not uncommon to find beaver dams flooding the roads and blocking the culverts. As road commissioner, my father had the task of destroying dams inflicting damage to the roads. It is impossible to take apart a dam with shovels and hoes, as they are an intricate weaving of sticks and logs. Dynamite was the chosen weapon against the large and inaccessible dams. We helped my father load the dynamite into the car together with the wires, caps, and a charger to ignite the dynamite. The culprit was a large beaver dam in the north end of Brookline flooding the road. A large family of beavers was busy extending the dam, cutting down trees, and tending their house. We placed charges along the base of the dam with strong wires to a small hillside overlooking the dam. From our vantage point, we had a good view of both the dam and the pond. My father let one of us ignite the dynamite. As we pushed down the plunger of the igniter, we suddenly saw the dam explode into the air; mud and sticks blew everywhere. Suddenly, the rush of water from the dam started flooding the brook. It did not take long for the beavers to notice a problem with their dam. As the level of the dam eroded, the access to the beaver house became visible. The adult beavers immediately started working repairing the dam. It was wonderful watching them work quickly on the repair, even the young beavers came out to help. I felt sorry that we found it necessary to destroy their carefully crafted work. When they started playing rather than working, one of the adults would swim up and slap them with his/her tail. It did not take the young ones long to get to work helping the adults. Ever so slowly, they started repairing the dam. We knew that it would take some time before the dam again created a problem.

FAKE BUTTER

IN the early 1950s, it was against the law to sell margarine in Vermont. This was the state's attempt to protect the dairy farmers. My uncle and father delivered lumber to Massachusetts and picked up cases of margarine on their return. The margarine was packaged in clear bags with a little color pill in the middle. You would squeeze the bag, breaking the pill and kneading the color throughout the package. It was the earliest margarine available on our table. For us with our dairy farm, it was a cheaper alternative to the butter my mother was forced to buy as we did not churn butter on the farm. Unfortunately, we did not associate the growth of margarine with lower dairy prices.

DISCOVERING THE ROBBERY

WE took of our Boy Scout trips to Frontier Town in New York. It was an amusement park trying to capture conditions from a different time. They staged a stagecoach robbery to the thrill of the young. One of our scout members, Freddy, decided to find out where the robbery was occurring. Freddy walked into the woods where the actors prepared for their play. Unfortunately, Freddy was discovered and shortly thereafter was brought aboard the stage to the center of the town where he was turned over to the scoutmasters. We were proud of Freddy and his detective work.

A LOT WENT ON WHEN THE BAND PLAYED!

SATURDAY'S main event in the summer was the Newfane Square Dance. It was held in the hay loft of an old barn outside of town. Every Saturday evening, Dick Perry and his band, with Ted Glayback calling, would entertain square dancers. It was the place to be on Saturday nights and the place where you made many new friends. You could hear the wonderful square dance music blaring down the highway as you drove past on route 30. Much went on outside and inside the hall. Beer was the drink of choice, either Schlitz or Budweiser. Many lives were created outside the hall on a Saturday evening. The resulting marriages were called "shotgun weddings."

TRYING TO FIND A BETTER HOME

I don't know why we ran away from home. We were about five and decided to walk to Newfane and find a better home. Maybe we were tired of weeding the garden or eating the portage that my mother served us for breakfast. One day we took off and started walking towards Newfane. In those days, there were not too many cars on the road. We probably walked two miles when we saw a car coming toward us. We hopped into the woods, but we were too late and were seen. It was our neighbor's mother coming to visit. She coaxed us into the car and drove us home. When she parked in our driveway, my mother came out of the house. We knew we were in trouble. As my mother was thanking Mrs. Whitney, we escaped from the car and ran into the house. The only safe place we could find was under my parent's bed. She stormed in the house and demanded we come out. We refused and she grabbed a broom handle and started hitting us under the bed. Finally, we came out and took our medicine and never ran away again.

DEMOCRATIC BROOKLINE WITH A SMALL "d"

MOST residents of Brookline were solidly Republican, but they were also democrats with a small "d." They were very accepting of people and ideas, as long as you did not tell them what to do. Our best teacher, Miss Watson, lived with the school bus driver Mary Beattie. They were a committed couple well before the world accepted open same-sex relationships. The town accepted them and their living arrangements. Another resident had a lesbian relationship with a neighbor who also had a boyfriend… again, although we children thought it a bit strange, not a word was said. There were affairs in town and probably much gossip behind the scenes, but nothing was said publicly. You could do what you wanted as long as you did not tell others how to live.

HORSES DELIVERED

MY Aunt who lived on the farm asked her NY City mother for horses for she and her friend. One day a horse trailer arrived at the farm with two riding horses and all the riding equipment. My mother and her friend teased her friend's mother. They wanted to know why they did not also receive riding horses. One day a trailer appeared outside my friend's house. A horsey man came to the door and told her the horses were in the van. My friends mother called my mother and asked her to come up to their house to see the horses. They did not know what they were going to do, for they did not have housing or feed for horses, nor did they really want horses. My mother and her friend went with the man to the trailer as he was telling them they were gentle horses and they would come to love them. He slowly opened the door of the trailer and sitting in the bed of hay were two bronze horses! My friends' mother had sent them two bronze horses in a horse trailer!

SUNDAY SCHOOL WITH THE MENNONITES

THE Baptist church in Brookline sits next to the grade school. The church was used for Christmas pageants and other gatherings. However, there was no minister, and church services were not regularly held. In the summer before we entered first grade, the Mennonites held Sunday school for the area youth in the church. I can still remember songs we sang and various activities. The Mennonite group only held school for a couple of summers and then moved on to another community. I am not sure if they saw us as a lost cause or there were better chances elsewhere.

SAP BEER IN THE CELLAR

OLD Vermonters, including my grandfather, made a sap beer at the end of the sugaring season. It was made from the last batch of sap with yeast and hops were added to create a pale beer. They placed the beer in a keg and stored it in the damp cellar to age. On a warm/hot July day, the men would break after work and consume some of the beer. All of us children would sneak down to the cellar on hot days and sip the beer. Although I am not a beer drinker, I have fond memories of the sap beer and how it tasted on a hot July day.

SNOWBALL FIGHTS IN JULY

IT did not snow in Vermont in July, but we had snowball fights. The sawdust from the lumber mill was blown into a big pile. When they operated the lumber mill in the winter, the sawdust would form a protective layer over the snow. The old times used sawdust in their ice houses for insulation! In the summer all you had to do was dig into the sawdust pile and find your own layer of snow. It was a great time of year for refreshing snowball fights and a surprise to visiting friends.

BRING THEM BACK, JESSIE AND HARLAN

MY parents were friends of a dairy couple in Windham, Vermont. They operated a small dairy farm in the center of the town. They had two children, a daughter and a son our age, named Alfred. Alfred had fifty pounds on each of us. When we visited the farm, Alfred would chase us around the barn and threaten to sit on us and do what else, we never knew. Fortunately, we were faster than Alfred, although he knew the barn better than we did and thus had that advantage. He would chase us around the barn and yell, "I'll get one of you and then watch out." When we left, he would say to my parents, "Bring them back, and next time, I'll catch one of them!" After leaving, we would beg my parents never bring us again.

KIDS SAY THE STRANGEST THINGS

IN the 1950s, the entertainer Art Linkletter interviewed children on live T.V. The responses were both cute and hilarious. I was home sick from school one day, and the television (black and white in those days) was turned on to the show. He was asking each of the children what they wanted for Christmas. One little boy said he wanted his own bed. Linkletter asked why he wanted his own bed. He said he normally slept in his mother's bed, and when his uncle came to visit, he had to sleep on the floor! I always wondered what the mother did to the boy after the show. It was live TV and what you saw was real in the moment conversation.

COUNTY INN AND JAIL

PRIOR to the 1970s, the county Inn and jail sat at the far end of Newfane Common and served those members serving in the county court system. They received room and board at the inn, and lunchtime meals were also available to the public. My friend's grandmother and grandfather, Mabel and Charlie Whitney, ran the Inn and county jail. The inmates were not hard-core; they were drunks or vagrants in need of a cooling-off period and time away from home. In exchange, the prisoners maintained the grounds and buildings. The hardcore convicts were sent up the river to Windsor. When we were at the inn/jail with our friend, the inmates gave us twenty-five cents to buy cigarettes at the local store with the understanding we could keep five cents to buy a popsicle. We made several trips to the store on a hot July and August days.

Mrs. Whitney squeeze a penny so hard it made Lincoln cry and she squeezed a nickel so hard the buffalo jumped! My mother and Mrs. Whitney's daughter Luna often waited on tables at the inn. When they recovered a plate from a diner with food remaining, it was scraped into a bowl and became the food served to the inmates. Charlie ran the jail, and one day, a new inmate decided to hitchhike to Brattleboro. Unknowingly, Charlie picked him up on the way to Brattleboro and gave him a ride to town.

One inmate was a regular and became part of the family. When the cold weather came, he did enough to find his home again in the jail. He was family with nowhere else to go. He was so trusted when my friend's parents needed a babysitter, they turned to him. He made himself an integral part of the family and they never locked the door on his jail cell. Such were the times at the Newfane county jail.

AID AT THE LOCAL LEVEL

TODAY, with the state mandates and requirements, little is left for local property tax appraisers. As a youth, I remember standing on my grandfather's milk house steps and listening to my grandfather and the other Brookline appraisers discuss their appraisals. They were reducing the annual appraisals on the house of a recent widow because she was poor. It was their way of providing some needed town assistance for those in need. There was no welfare system to help those in need.

DAVID BEING WIRETAPPED

MY older brother David lived in Hebron, Connecticut and became heavily involved in the McCarthy presidential campaign. I am not sure when he became a rabid Democrat, but he showed his colors when he joined that campaign. One day, he stopped at the local gas station and was told a man had asked for directions to his house a few days earlier. David became suspicious and went down to his cellar to find his phone had been tapped. Such was the times in the late sixties when the anti-war activities were occurring against the Vietnam war and Nixon was President.

FIRST TV IN TOWN

OUR neighbors owned the first TV in Brookline given to them by their grandmother It was a big-boxed device with a hexagonal screen. The signal was not strong and was provided by a large antenna in the yard. The picture was rather hazy and hard to see. However, it did not stop us from watching "Howdy Doodie," "Buffalo Bob" and "Clara Bell the Clown." We knew all the characters. We also watched the musketeers and some other shows we did not understand. The screen was so small we had to crowd around to watch the black and white screen. Our channel choices and shows were few.

CHAPTER 6

FAMILY

DRIVING TURKEYS TO BOSTON

WE spent time with my father and grandfather in the barn during milking. My grandfather would tell tales of his grandfather and others. His grandfather and others drove turkeys to Boston where other animals would also be driven to market. The feet of the turkeys would be tarred to protect them on the trip.

CRUISING TIMBER LOTS

MY father and uncle owned a lane lumber mill. The mill was state of the art in the 1950s with an edger and end clippers to size the boards. They owned approximately 700 acres of land the periodically harvest. They also bought timber and logs from other landowners. We often accompanied my father when he went to look at those other timber lots. He would refer to the practice as "cruising the timber lot". He quickly surveyed the lot to determine the approximate board feet of timber available and the quality of that timber.

GERMAN LOVED VERMONT

AFTER I left the navy and was married, my wife and I traveled to Germany to visit my twin brother and his wife. Roger was serving in the army and did not have much free time. My wife, his wife and I decided to take a trip through parts of Germany, Switzerland, and Austria. I took enough German in college to get by, but I certainly was not fluent. We went into a small restaurant in Germany, and an elderly couple asked me if I, with my blond hair, was from Holland. I told them I was from the United States.

They asked me where, and I told them New England. They asked me where in New England, and I told them Vermont. Their eyes lit up and a smile came to their face. They told me their son was in a labor camp in Vermont during World War II and he loved Vermont. There was a small labor camp near the Trapp Family lodge during World War II. It was better than the Russian Front!

(ATH)ens or (A)thens

THE town to the north of Brookline is called (ATH)ens. My twin brother was working with the Vermont Historian who did not grow up in Vermont. Rog mentioned he grew up in the town next to (ATH)ens. The historian corrected him and said it was pronounced (A)thens. Whereupon, Roger told him in (A)thens it might be (A)thens, but in (ATH)ens, it was pronounced (ATH)ens!

SHE IS AWFULLY DARK, ISN'T SHE?

IT was the late 1960s and my new wife and I went to Connecticut to visit my elderly grandparents. My grandmother grew up in Brattleboro, Vermont and had moved to Connecticut later in life with her second husband. My wife was part Spanish and worked as a lifeguard and swimming instructor during the summer. She would tan easily and would become quite dark. After the introductions, my grandmother grabbed me and took me into another room. She said, "She's awfully dark, isn't she?" I told her she was, and it really did not matter to me!

GETTING A BULL OUT OF A RING

MY wife and I traveled to Spain and spent a couple of days in Madrid. Neither of us had seen a bullfight, and one of the premier fights was being held at the Madrid Arena. The king's mother was the honored guest, and some of the most famous matadors in Spain were challenging the bulls. We watched as one bull after another was tested and finally dragged away dead from the ring. Finally, a special bull appeared and was undaunted with all they did to him. The bull was obviously a star, and the king's mother decided the bull should be saved. How do you get a mad bull out of the ring? First, they sent in several matadors who ended up jumping over the fence away from the charging bull. They then sent in some heifers hoping the bull would follow them from the ring. He was not interested in any females that evening! They then sent in a little dog to chase the bull. It did not take long for the little dog to scoot out of the ring. After about one hour, they were able to coax the bull from the arena. The matadors finally enticed the exhausted bull from the ring.

AMERICAN LEGION PARADE IN BARRE

BARRE, Vermont is a small industrial town in Central Vermont known for its granite industry and a statue of Bobby Burns on the lawn of the former high school. Often, the statue would have a can of beer in its hand! My father-in-law was the commander of the American Legion, and annually, they would hold a Memorial Day parade. My children were between 5 and 8 at the time, and we would take them every year to the parade to watch the legionnaire's march. Most of the participants served in either World War II or the Korean Conflict. The parade always started at the north end of town and went down Main Street toward the American Legion. My son asked why they marched toward the legion and not up Main Street. I told him it was important for the legionnaires to get to the bar quickly! It was not an unfair assessment as my father-in-law and others loved their beer!

WHAT DID YOU DO IN THE WAR?

ANNUALLY, my friend Jules, my brother-in-law and I would travel to Island Pond, Vermont to fish. Island Pond had been a railroad town and was then a large logging center. Jules served honorably as a tail gunner in World War II flying over Germany. He did not talk about his war experiences, but the survival rate was not large. One evening after fishing, we decided to visit the local American Legion located in the center of town. We were enjoying our drinks when a large logger stopped by our table to talk. Jules was could befriend anyone, and before long, he was bantering freely with the guy. Jules asked what he did in the service. The man said he was the legion commander, and he stayed stateside and was a cook. Jules started jeering him about being a cook and not seeing action. The man was not happy and whistled to some of his logging friends to come over and take us out! I jumped under the table as Jules started to calm things down. After a few minutes with no punches thrown, things calmed down. Jules started buying everyone drinks. Before we left, Jules asked if they ever went to Barre, Vermont. They said they often visited Barre. Jules told them to go into the legion and have drinks on John Anderson who was commander of the Barre legion. John was Jules' brother-in-law and my father-in-law. We never did learn if drinks were placed on John's tab.

CHURCH FINANCE COMMITTEE

MY first wife and I lived in Barre, Vermont. She worked at Norwich University and I worked for the state of Vermont in various capacities. We became active in the Congregational church. I was asked to join the finance committee. Not only was the committee in charge of church finances, but it was also charged with raising money each year through pledge campaigns. Barre was famous for its granite industry, and several of those prominent families were members of the church. I learned those who had the money gave very little, and those with very little gave much more. It was always a struggle to raise sufficient money to maintain the church and pay its minister. He was my age with a nice sense of humor. At one meeting, while discussing the fundraiser, I suggested half-jokingly to Rich the church should charge for its services. I said, "You hatch them, patch them, match them and dispatch them. You should charge accordingly."

SPANISH TRAINS

SHORTLY after my first wife and I were married, we traveled to Santander, Spain to visit her relatives. I was serving as acting commissioner of agriculture and we visited her relatives farm in the hills near the town. The women went out in the morning and cut the hay with scythes and brought it in with donkey carts. The men milked the few cows by hand. Judith told them I was the secretary of agriculture for Vermont. They interpreted it as though I was the secretary of agriculture for the United States, as they had no idea where Vermont was. They called me "El Rubio" or the blond one, and it was not long before the expensive wine was pulled out from under the sink, and we all had a good time.

We were to travel from Santander to the capital of Spain, Madrid. We went to the railroad station, and it was evident that we had to change trains. I asked my wife who asked the station manager, and he insisted that the train took us directly to Madrid. However, I could read maps. We got on the train and traveled for several hours when the train stopped at a station. We stayed on the train, and as it started up, a conductor came through the train. He looked at our tickets and pulled the stop cord ordering us off the train with our baggage. We are about one mile out of the station and had to hike back. My wife asked when the next train to Madrid was coming through, and they told us in about five hours. We went to the Tapa Bar and the stationmaster came in and told us there was a Madrid train coming. We went out and saw a World War II transport train coming from Portugal with Portuguese workers hanging out the windows... half drunk. We boarded, and the only space was between the train cars in the restroom area. There were already three Portuguese workers drinking wine sitting there. We sat on our suitcases and they offered us some of their wine. They threw their wine bottles at the sheep as we passed through sheep country. . It was a tiring, but exciting ride to Madrid as another bottle was found and another good bottle of wine was enjoyed.

I LIKED HIS DOG

MY son's best friend in high school was Matt. Matt's grandfather had served as a Supreme Court justice and was famous for saying that "he could not define pornography, but he knew it when he saw it." My son was invited to travel with Matt to Washington and stay at his grandmother's. The Bushes and the Stewarts were longtime friends. While there, they went out to the vice president's residence to have tea with Barbara Bush. The boys were on the floor playing with Millie the dog when the vice president came back from campaigning for the presidency. When he walked into the room, Matt's grandmother motioned for the boys to stand up and greet the vice president. When David arrived home, I asked him what he thought, for he might well have shaken the hand of the next president of the United States and what an honor it was for a boy of his age. He told me was he thought the vice president had a nice dog."

WHO KILLED THOSE ANIMALS?

WHEN my daughter Elizabeth was about seven, I took her to Washington We visited the Museum of Natural History with its life-sized African animals on display in their natural habitat. When she seven-and-a-half years old, she wrote a letter to the animal protection fund in which she stated, "I hope I could help, but I'm only seven-and-a-half years old. For now, I will just give you $4. It might not be much, but I just want to help. When I grow up, I want to be a vet." She wanted to know who killed the animals and whom she could talk to about the animals. I told her we should visit another museum as I knew she would not be satisfied with what they told her about the dead animals.

THAT'S MY SON

I was serving as Vermont's Secretary of Agriculture, and my son had just received his driver's license. He was driving our car with my low license number to pick up his friend in Dummerston. The roads in Dummerston were newly plowed and sanded, yet slippery in places. He picked up his friend and was starting down a hill when he lost control of the car. The car was skidding and heading toward another car. The woman in the other car recognized my son and the passenger, and said, "That's my son headed toward us." The cars collided just as she finished her statement. Fortunately, only the cars were damaged and there were no injuries. The state police were called to the scene. The policeman took down all the pertinent information, came back to the car and said to my son, "Your Dad is Secretary of Agriculture and he is going to be pissed!" I was not angry, but happy no one was injured. A vehicle could be fixed.

THE DEA IS WATCHING!

MY stepson majored in religion and plant and soil science at the University of Vermont. He was still finding himself when he stayed with us one summer in Essex, New York. We ran a bed and breakfast and maintained a large organic produce garden. I informed him he could grow all the plants he wanted off the property. Every day he would follow his trail off the property to tend the plants. When he was away one day, I followed his path and placed a printed card on each plant that said, "inspected by the DEA." When he next visited his plants, he came back ashen faced. I finally told him the truth.

WATCHING A TEACHER BEAT A STUDENT

I am not sure when it happened, but we became an unruly group of students. I believe it occurred after Miss Watson and Miss Gordon retired. They brought in a temporary teacher with experience dealing with difficult students. One day a difficult boy called her names and caused other difficulties. Mrs. F, the temporary teacher, grabbed the student by the cuff of the neck and dragged him outside to the side of the school where we could all watch. She started beating him until he promised to behave in the future. There was never a problem with another student during her tenure at the school. Not only was she a disciplinarian with a great right hook, but she was also a good teacher. Today, a teacher would be fired under similar circumstances.

After Miss Gordon and Miss Watson retired, we "tried" many teachers. Miss Leo from Winooski was the first I remembered. She fit in very well but became homesick and returned to northern Vermont. Miss D was the second teacher from Rutland, Vermont and a recent graduate of a teacher's college. I can't remember exactly what caused me to dislike to her, but I took a total dislike to her. Perhaps, because she favored some students over others or because she was inconsistent in how she taught. I made life difficult for her when I was presented with the opportunity. She finally had enough of my actions and took me into a private room for a conference. She knew that I loved fishing and came up with a novel approach. If I behaved, she would have her father, a fisherman, take me along on a fishing trip. If I did not behave, she was going to send me to the reform school in Vergennes, Vermont where they were accustomed to handling students like me. In no uncertain terms, I told her to send me to reform school as I did not want to go fishing with her father. I thought to myself the tree nut could not be too much different than the tree it came from. Fortunately, my parents were not prepared to see me shipped away, and I improved during the remaining school year. Miss D finished out her year and moved on to another school.

TEACHING SUNDAY SCHOOL CONFIRMATION CLASS

MY wife and I were very active in the Congregational church in Barre, Vermont. One year they were without a Sunday school teacher for the confirmation class. They kept pressuring me to teach, and I kept resisting until I was worn down. The students were very difficult eighth graders who wanted to be somewhere else and only attended due to parental pressure. I tried to teach them about the Bible and bring in some relevance. My final effort was to have them make wreaths, which would be delivered to area nursing and care homes. They even fought me on that effort. I was at my wit's end. I traveled regularly to Boston on energy matters. I went into a bookstore where I purchased a book on making paper airplanes. At the next class, I told them whoever could produce the best airplane would win the book. We had quite a contest, and I handed out the book to the winner. It was the end of my Sunday school career and I was never invited back!

PI AND WHERE IS MY GIN

MY stepson and his girlfriend graduated from the University of Vermont We decided to hold a graduation party at our bed and breakfast in Essex, New York. My stepmother-in-law loved her gin and kept a half gallon of it in the pantry, which she visited quite frequently. The party was catered with a local person cooking and serving the wines. I noticed my stepmother-in-law drank a glass of wine and headed to the pantry and chased it down with her gin. She kept doing this all evening. I was not worried because she knew how to hold her liquor. The next morning, she confronted me and wanted to know who was drinking her gin because the bottle was almost empty. I told her she had consumed the gin the previous evening . She had forgotten about her drinking and the party.

DAVID AND SEMINARY

MY son entered a Catholic seminary in Maryland following graduation from the University of Vermont. He became a covert to the Catholic faith while at the University of Vermont. It was a very conservative seminary and he sometimes complained about the conservatism of fellow students.

I told him he would find difficult people wherever he was; the test was to find a way to work successfully with all types. He told me a story about a parish priest who taught part-time at the seminary. One day, the priest arrived in a brand-new car. One of the students said, "Father, you take a vow of poverty. How can you purchase a new car?" The priest replied, "Fuck you." On another occasion, the same priest went to visit an elderly parishioner. The priest was rather rotund and when he sat down as she was getting him tea, he sat on her small dog and killed it. He quickly put the dead dog in his pocket and said nothing. On the way home, he opened the window and chucked the dog outside!

I HOPE HE DOESN'T LOOK LIKE THAT

MY stepson attended Reed College, a very progressive liberal arts college in Portland, Oregon. His mother and grandmother flew out to visit during his freshman year. They rented a car and drove to campus and parked outside one of the administrative/lecture halls. They watched many students and marveled at the dress or lack thereof. They noticed one student dressed in rags with a full beard. While he fit into the student landscape, he was the worst dressed of the group. My wife turned to her mother and said, "I hope my son doesn't look like that!" The student approached the car, and my wife recognized the student in rags as her son! He was living in a house with a hole in the floor, a pet pig, and a python snake missing in the walls!

CHAPTER 7

EDUCATION

THE Brookline Grade School was a two-room structure built adjacent to the Baptist church. The second room addition was added after the war to house all the "war babies." During our last years at the school, the student population had fallen to a level where only one room was utilized. Following graduation, we attended Leland and Gray Seminary, a poor private school in Townshend which served the valley students. We then enrolled at the University of Vermont. Following the navy, I enrolled in the graduate program at the University of Connecticut.

COWS IN SCHOOL WINDOW AND FIRST LOVE

THE Brookline school was surrounded on two sides by school property. Directly in back was Lester Rink's cow pasture. In the warm spring and on fall days, the back-school windows were opened and once in a while a cow would stick her head into the class room. The school had started and Judy, a first grader from the north end, would arrive around 8:15 a.m. I would go over and help her take off her coat and give her a good morning kiss. My actions were quickly stopped. The teacher said a public display of affection was inappropriate and not allowed in school. Unfortunately, my first true love moved away, and it would be years before I found another girlfriend.

High School

LELAND and Gray Seminary in Townshend, Vermont was started as a private high school in the 1800s by the Baptist Church. It was still a private school when we were enrolled and no longer associated with the Baptist. The school served students throughout the West River Valley. . The school took a prominent and beautiful position on the common until the 1970s when it was torn down to build a regional high school. What the school lacked in facilities it made up with its teachers and their commitment to education.

MY BOYS ARE GOING TO COLLEGE

MY mother took us to meet the headmaster to register for our courses prior to our freshman year at Leland and Gray. Arlo was one of those headmasters who did everything... he taught, he coached, and he managed the school. Here were two boys coming from a farming family which also operated a sawmill. I am sure Arlo thought we might someday return to that way of life when he suggested courses we might take our freshman year. He told my mother we should consider the general level courses as well as shop classes. That was enough for my mother. She said, "Mr. Monroe, you don't understand; my sons are going to college and not returning to the farm or lumber mill." With that, Arlo did understand, and we enrolled in college level courses.

SLEEP WELL TONIGHT

WHEN you drive along Vermont highways, it is difficult to believe those highways once held billboards. The billboard legislation was passed in the early 1970s and permanently phased out billboards in Vermont. When we were in high school, there was a billboard to the south of Townshend which contained a National Guard advertisement. It said, "Sleep well tonight, your National Guard is awake." Several of our classmates joined the National Guard in their senior year, and they told us about their weekends. We painted over part of the billboard so it said, "Sleep well tonight, your National Guard Is!" Unlike today, the National Guard in those days was called out for floods and other emergencies.

FINDING BEER IN THE BROOK

WE were all freshmen at Leland and Gray Seminary. Although beer was available, it was against the law being caught with it if you were under twenty-one. Of course, as freshmen, we were no more than fourteen or fifteen. One of our classmates was caught by the police with beer and was summoned to appear in court. When the judge asked him where he obtained the beer, not wanting to squeal on his source, he said, "I found it in the brook when I was fishing." Unfortunately, he and the judge were well aware fishing season had yet to start. He received a misdemeanor and a fine.

TWIN DISCRIMINATION

OUR class was a small class of 20 students. Rog and I were excellent students who participated in many sports and other activities. Every year two junior boys were chosen to attend "Boys State" in Montpelier, Vermont. It was a week of activities where the formed and managed a democratic government. They chose two male students not active or involved in student activities. After the choice, we learned we were not chosen because they thought it unfair to the other students to send two of us and unfair to each of us if they chose one of us. It was blatant discrimination; were we from different families each of us would have been chosen!

THEY DIDN'T LIKE BEING BEATEN!

LELAND and Gray was a poor country high school serving mostly poor rural children. The school did its best with the little money available. Dave was our soccer and skiing coach who coached with a passion. We did not possess light balsa wood cross-country skis Our skis were made from old World War II army surplus skis cut down to cross-country ski size. Our skis were heavier and difficult to track in snow. However, we put our hearts into the effort. Cross-country skis are waxed based on the snow conditions. The goal was to put a wax on which helps hill climbing and assists slides going down. A purist measures snow and weather conditions and applies appropriate waxes. We and other schools were invited to compete against Putney School, an excellent team possessing the latest ski equipment. Their coach later went on to become the American Olympic cross-country ski coach. Prior to the race, Putney skiers were putting their thermometers in the snow to select the best wax. We, on the other hand, looked at the snow and the proposed weather conditions and slapped a couple of waxes on our old and cumbersome cut down army skis. Putney was ahead for the first half of the race, and it looked like we would come in last. Suddenly, the weather changed, and their wax no longer worked. The wax we just randomly applied worked like a charm, and we passed them with ease. We, with our outlandish cross-country skis, finished the race well ahead of any Putney students or other teams. I remember their coach's anger when our rag tag team from the poor school beat his expensively equipped students, coached by one of the best!

WHAT NOT TO DO IN SCHOOL!

MY brother and I would be serving time in jail today for our offenses. When we were growing up, the purchase of dynamite and other incendiary material was possible. It was a different time and blowing things up was not part of the ordinary life. Roger and I were making little bombs we set off apart from other people. They were dangerous if not handled properly. Unfortunately, we told one of our classmates how to make the devices. He proudly came to school with all the elements needed for the bombs. We directed him to take the materials home and forget about making the devices. He assured us the material would go home with him at the end of the day. We were relieved he made the promise. It was a nice October day and we were playing soccer when we heard a loud explosion. A few minutes later, our friend struggled to the school bleeding terribly with shrapnel wounds throughout his body. He was taken to the hospital where shrapnel was removed from his body, some narrowly missing his privates. Fortunately, he quickly recovered with no permanent damage to his body. He was removed from school for a couple of weeks and did not tell the authorities where he received his bomb-making instructions. Twenty years later at a high school reunion our classmates were discussing the injury to the student. They were surprised to learn my brother and I had provided the prior instructions.

NOT A GOOD MARINE

DAVID, our older brother, married the daughter of a World War II Marine General who led troops in the Iwa Jimma battle. His in-laws had three daughters, and the middle daughter, Adele, followed her father into the Marines. Adele would often visit my brother and his wife in Newfane.

It was 1962 or 1963, and we were just learning about some far Asian country in the news. During one visit, she was accompanied by a male Marine Captain who returned from advisory duty in Vietnam. We were young and ending our high school career and didn't fully understand where Vietnam was located or his role in that country. He regaled us with stories about his service in Vietnam. He was there helping the South Vietnamese government combat the communists and the Viet Cong. It was an opportunity to fight communism, and he was proud to be part of that effort. He talked about capturing insurgent Viet Cong and extracting critical information from them. He regaled us in how he treated the Viet Cong who were captured. They would take prisoners up in a helicopter and ask about troop movements and locations. Two or three would be airlifted at one time. The first, refusing to answer questions, was thrown out of the helicopter. The second or third prisoner was always answering his questions, and they too would be tossed out! That marine provided our first real exposure to an active duty soldier serving in a combat zone and some of the early atrocities.

College Years

WE both enrolled as liberal arts students at the University of Vermont in 1963. During our sophomore years, we switched to the College of Agriculture, but continued to take most of our courses in the Liberal Arts. The University was still small with no more than 6,000 students. However, it was a big jump for us going from a student body of 120 to 6000. After the service, I enrolled in the University of Connecticut and obtained my master's degree.

HOW TO TELL THE SEX OF A COW

ROGER and I were accepted at the University of Vermont in the college of liberal arts. We elected to switch to the College of Agriculture and major in agricultural and resource economics our sophomore year. Although we continued to take many courses in the liberal arts, it allowed us to take applied courses related to agriculture. Unfortunately, there were some basic courses required of all majors in the College of Agriculture. One course was entitled Farm Management and consisted of both classroom time and farm tours related to the management of dairy and other farm enterprises. Some of the students were fresh off city streets and were enrolled in the college as pre-veterinary students. Unlike my brother and I, they had never set foot in a dairy barn, and their only contact with a cow was through a storybook. We were taking a tour of a farm and were walking past the ass end of some heifers. One of the pre-vet students quietly asked us, "How do you tell the sex of a cow?" We told him the only sure way of telling the sex of a cow was to stand in front of the cow and look it squarely in the eyes. If it blinked, it was male. If it did not blink, it was a female. He took us seriously and walked around to the front of the heifers to stare them in the eyes.

WHEN ARE YOU GOING TO GET A HAIRCUT?

WHEN my wife and I were attending graduate school in Storrs, Connecticut, my grandparents lived nearby. I often went over to help paint or paper their house. My grandparents were regular church attendees and had a picture of the last supper on their wall. One day as I was painting inside, my grandmother asked me when I was going to get a haircut. My hair was not very long, but she thought I had waited too long. I turned to the picture and told her I would get a haircut when Jesus cut his hair. She never bothered me about a haircut again.

OPPORTUNITY TO VISIT MY GIRLS!

IT was the summer of my junior year at the University of Vermont. I needed a break from a summer in Brookline and signed up for an internship with the Farmers Home Administration in Rutland, Vermont. The Farmers Home Administration was a service of USDA and provided both direct and guaranteed loans to farmers and some small rural businesses in Vermont. I thought Rutland a good choice since it was only two hours away from home and would be livelier than Brookline or Newfane. As a single young male, I was looking for a little independence and excitement. My supervisor in Rutland was a young Maine potato farmer's son, and he not only took me under his wings, but also went out of his way to introduce me to many of the farmers FMHA served. One day, as I was sitting in the office looking over some loan documents, a farmer from Wallingford walked in. He introduced himself and asked me a few questions. Finally, he said, "Bet you would like to meet my daughters?" As a single young man, images of healthy and attractive young farmwomen danced through my head. I told him I would love to meet his daughters. He seemed quite pleased. I finally asked how many daughters he had. He said he had at least forty. I realized he was talking about his cows and had no daughters. My disappointment showed and he enjoyed his joke.

YOU CAUCASIONS LOOK ALIKE!

A Chinese American professor taught a popular graduate school mathematics course at UCONN. During our first class, he looked around the room as he was calling our names. He said, "You will have to excuse me, it will take some time for me to recognize each of you because all white people look alike!"

GIVING ADVICE AS A STORE CLERK

AFTER the navy and before the start of graduate school, I worked at Lord and Taylor in West Hartford, Connecticut. I was newly married and working in the men's department. It was the holiday season and people were buying presents for their loved ones. A very proper lady told me her granddaughter was recently married and she was there to buy pajamas for her granddaughter's new husband. Could I direct her to a nice pair of pajamas? She further asked me if I thought it would be a nice present for a newly married couple. I suggested she either buy him a shirt or tie!

Another rather wealthy woman came in to buy items for her around-the-world cruise. She was gushing about her planned cruise... almost bragging. I informed her I just came back from such a cruise a year earlier. She inquired further, and I told her about my visits to Japan, Hong Kong, Sydney, Rio, and Wellington. I did not mention we stopped for several months while carrying out operations in Vietnam!

IF YOU FAIL MY COURSE, YOU WILL BE THERE!

ONE of the more popular courses for liberal art students at the university was International Politics taught by Professor Gould. His course was popular due not only to its subject matter, but due to his teaching abilities. Vietnam was always in the news, and premiers of Vietnam were always changing. Professor Gould would pepper the class with questions about the news and the implications for the country. Many sports jocks sat in the very back of the class hoping that Professor Gould would not call on them. One day, he asked one of the players the name of the new premier of South Vietnam. The athlete clearly did not know the answer. Professor Gould said he had better find out because he would be over there fighting when he flunked his course.

HAVEN'T I SEEN YOU BEFORE?

ROTC was required during our freshman and sophomore years at UVM. Two morning classes were devoted to curriculum, and one class either Friday or Saturday was devoted to drills. Roger's drill was Friday morning, and my drill was on a Saturday. Toward the end of the semester, we were graded on our drills as well as the curriculum. For some reason, I could not make my drill test and persuaded my brother to take my test for me. On Friday he took his test and was graded by a black sergeant. On Saturday he took the same test and was graded by the same sergeant. The sergeant said, "Man, haven't I seen you somewhere before?" My brother did not respond and received a higher grade for me than he did for himself.

WHAT IS COOKING IN THE FRATERNITY'S OVEN?

I earned part of my room and board washing dishes at my fraternity. There were no automatic dishwashers and all dishes were washed by hand. Our fraternity cook was a wonderful woman named Del. She used about every pot and pan in the fraternity when cooking. She and I enjoyed each other's company, and I would always chide her about using too many pots and pans. It was always a challenge to find all the dirty posts and pans, as she was not above hiding some. I came in to wash dishes one day and started my pots and pan hunt. I opened the oven door to see if they were hidden there and found a pair of her panties drying. She evidently wet them and washed and dried them in the stove. She was very embarrassed I found them.

I REMEMBER WHERE I WAS
WHEN KENNEDY WAS KILLED!

IN the fall of 1963, I was just finishing my German class when I heard a commotion outside in the hall. Students were gathered, and someone was announcing the president had been shot. A short time later, it was announced the president was dead from a gunshot in Dallas. College was cancelled and we all returned home to grieve. It was a shock to the nation, but a real shock to my generation who saw youth and vitality in the president. Our family gathered at the home of our friends in Brattleboro, Robert and Luna Howe. We were watching the news when Oswald was brought out of the jail. We, as well as thousands of others, watched as Jack Ruby shot and killed Oswald. With that shot, our knowledge of why and if anyone else was behind the shooting disappeared. Lyndon Johnson once said the country would be in turmoil if they learned the truth about the assignation.

A TERRIBLE LOSS

ALL healthy male students were required to enroll in Army ROTC during their first two years at the University. Captain Strickler, was one of the regular captain instructors during our freshmen year. I remember him as a very polished officer who would succeed in the army. He left us during our sophomore year and was sent to Vietnam. It was 1965, and the war was escalating . We received news he was killed on a barge in the Saigon River a few months later. Evidently, he was shot by a sniper. It was our first sense of loss of a man who should have lived a full and productive life and most likely would have become a general.

PROFESSOR ANASAWARI AND INTERNATIONAL ECONOMICS

TWINSHIP has its advantage in many situations. Professor Anaswari was an Iraqi economics professor who taught international economics. We took his class our junior year. Participation in the class was a significant factor in your final grade. We knew he could not tell us apart, and by constantly changing our seating, he was confused. We also took turns preparing for class so he could not always tell which Allbee was actively participating. We each received an "A" for the class.

THIS IS MY RIFLE AND THIS IS MY GUN, SERGEANT

ONLY unhealthy freshman and sophomore students were exempted from ROTC classes at the University of Vermont. We were provided with army uniforms and a carbine at enrollment. Our first ROTC class our freshman year was quite intimidating. We were given World War II rifles and instructed in close order drills. Unlike my brother and I, many of the other students had never handled a gun. Our first instructor was a man named Sergeant Benway. He bore more WWII medals on his chest than Carter has liver pills. I can still hear the Sergeant standing in front of us and yelling… "This is my rifle, this is my gun, this is for shooting, and this is for fun!" He was intent on making a soldier out of each student. He obviously saw action in World War II and Korea.

POSTCARDS AND GRADES

IN the 1960s, college grades were not a private matter. Professors routinely posted student's grades on bulletin boards for all to see. In my first economics course, after an hour exam, the professor walked into the room, wrote the number of students earning each grade on the bulletin board, and started handing out the grades in that order. Fortunately, I always did extremely well in economics, so everyone knew that I received one of the highest grades. At the end of the year, we would provide our professors with postcards, and they would send our grades home with a note on the postcard. Since we knew our postmaster read every postcard, we decided to have fun. We made out a postcard to ourselves, gave us an "F," and noted we were such difficult students the professor never again wanted to see us in his class. After that time, whenever we went into the post office to pick up mail, the postmaster would give us a strange look. Our parents also received the postcards and were immediately angered by what they read. We had some explaining to do.

CHICKENS IN THE HALL AND A COW IN THE LOUNGE

MY brother and I were housed in Chittenden Hall during our freshman year at the University of Vermont. I woke up one morning to the smell of cow manure and heard chickens running up and down our hall. In the 1960s, the UVM farm was on the hill behind the dorms. Someone had the bright idea of leading one of the big Holsteins into the Chittenden lounge and releasing some chickens in the halls. Unfortunately, they were able to get the Holstein into the dorm, but had a difficult time leading her out. In the process, she decided to unload everything she had in her… and what a mess it made. The Dean of Students was called to the dorm and threatened to put everyone on probation, even those of us not involved in the stunt. All hands were called to clean up duty to avoid probation. It took some time for the smell to evaporate from the dorm.

TV FOR THE BEATLES

TODAY, it is hard to believe the University of Vermont dorms had no TVs in 1963. Most students were die-hard music fans, and we learned the Beatles would perform on the Ed Sullivan Show on a Sunday night. My dorm purchased a TV - we each chipped in $10.00 and charged non-dorm attendees a fee to watch the show. The room filled up quickly that Sunday evening, with those of us who helped purchase the TV receiving reserved seats. It was a packed audience watching the soon-to-be famous group play on the Ed Sullivan show that Sunday evening. We had a dorm TV paid for by other students.

YOU MEN NEED TO STUDY!

TEACHERS and professors could get away with much in the 1960s. During my sophomore year at the University, I enrolled in Economics 101 The class was composed of both male and female students. At the first class, the professor told the male students the only way they would succeed in his class was by studying hard. He told the female students they need not study. He said females had long understood economics, and therefore, studying was unnecessary! Today, he would be fired for making such statements.

NAVY RECRUITER

DURING the summer of my last two college years, I painted the interior of houses for Walt Tarbell. Walt's full-time worker was Oscar Plumley who spent years during WWII on a submarine. Oscar told me he spent seventeen months at sea without seeing land. Oscar was a gifted man, and he and I had many enjoyable times together. Oscar enjoyed kidding around, and one day I called the navy recruiter and asked him to visit. I gave him Oscar's address and telephone number. A few days later, Oscar was visited by the recruiter. Oscar enjoyed the moment, and I'm sure he gave the recruiter some good navy stories.

FRENCH 45

STUDENTS at the University of Vermont and other universities can now take a pass-fail in a course not counting toward their average. They also receive a letter grade rather than a number grade. When my twin brother and I were at the University of Vermont, you received a number grade for your course. We were required to take a language course during our first two years at the university. Although I had taken French at Leland and Gray, I knew the French course in high school was subpar and would not provide any advantage in college French. I choose German and succeeded in the courses. My twin brother let them sign him up for French II since he had high school French. Roger really struggled in the course and ended up with a grade of 45... so we told people he was enrolled in College French 45.

ROUTE 66 SEQUENCE IN BROOKLINE

ROUTE 66 was a popular 1960s TV show. It involved two young men who drove a Corvette to different parts of the country and solved problems. In 1967, the show was filmed in Brookline/Newfane, Vermont and my father was hired to provide equipment and background equipment for the show. I think it was one of the more exciting things to happen in Brookline and many of the residents were paid extras.

CHAPTER 8

SERVICE

WE were brought up with relatives and neighbors who had returned from World War II and the Korean War. We were expected to serve our country. When the Vietnam conflict escalated and young men and women were needed, we did not consider not serving. We knew little about Asia or the politics leading up to the conflict. We were quite ignorant of history and were ready to follow the leaders of our country. We were taught to trust and believe our leaders. As the conflict escalated, we began to understand the futility of the conflict and the losses which occurred. My twin continued with army ROTC and was commissioned a second lieutenant upon graduation. I enrolled in the navy and took training at OCS in Newport, Rhode Island. The classes were filled with young men who wanted to avoid the draft, but were still willing to serve their country.

Navy vs. Army

YOU CAN CHANGE BRANCHES OF THE SERVICE

ROGER was commissioned a second lieutenant in the army following completion of ROTC at the university. I chose Navy OCS and was commissioned as an ensign in the navy, the equivalent of an Army second lieutenant. Roger was sent to the Aberdeen Proving Ground in Maryland to study army missiles. Following OCS, I was sent to Sandia Base in New Mexico to study nuclear weapons. Sandia Base served as a training base for all the services. The first few weeks all branches trained together and were then separated to study the weapons tailored to their branch of service. I arrived in Albuquerque wearing my white naval uniform and was checking into the base. At the same time, a young army second lieutenant was checking in, and he looked at me with some questions on his face. He finally said, "What are you doing in a navy uniform? I saw you at Aberdeen in an army uniform two weeks ago?" I told him it was true, but the army was losing too many second lieutenants in Vietnam and I changed services. I told him he could take advantage of the opportunity if he wished. He said no and left for his barracks. We ended up in the same training group, and I told him it was my identical twin brother he saw in the army uniform.

I DECIDED TO TAKE THE DAY OFF

ROGER served in a small unit supplying nuclear weapons to the British. It was a very small base overseen by a lieutenant colonel. Roger said the lieutenant colonel had an attitude and made life difficult on the base. I imagine my brother made life difficult for him at times. After I left the navy, my wife and I traveled to Germany to visit my brother and his new wife, Ann. Roger and Ann picked us up at the airport, and we drove north to his small base. When we arrived on base, I went to the PX to change dollars into Germany money. As I was standing at the window, the lieutenant colonel approached and said, "Allbee, where have you been today, I did not give you authority to leave." I replied, "Colonel, I don't care what you think, I took the day off!" He huffed, got red in the face, and said he would take care of me later. He left the post and immediately ran into my brother wearing his army uniform!

THE SIXTH SENSE

PEOPLE did not possess cell phones in the late 1960s. When away from home, you found the nearest pay phone. My brother was stationed at the Aberdeen proving grounds, and I was stationed in Albuquerque, New Mexico. Roger and I did not call nor write letters to each other while in the service; perhaps, it was because of our innate ability to sense the other. Periodically, perhaps once a month, I would call home. He would also call home about once per month. They later informed us whenever one of us called, the other would call within the hour. So much for telepathy or twin communication.

SHIT FLOATS AND JUST JUMP INTO THE OCEAN

WE were sitting around our table with our college friends in Brookline, enjoying the summer before we went off to the service. It was a nice leisurely meal when a neighbor's son barged in and told us he was going to enlist and could not wait to kill a few Vietnamese. He was a little crazy, but we had no doubt the army would take him. We said he would not have any trouble getting to that country since shit floated and all he had to do was jump in the ocean and the current would carry him to his destination. He was unfazed over our suggestion and continued ranting about killing the Vietnamese!

KILLING THE SYMBOL OF PEACE

WE were cruising slightly more than twelve miles off the coast of North Vietnam. Looking out the doors of the hanger bay, we could clearly see the mountains of the country in the not too far distance. We were between air operations on the U.S.S. *America*, and I, a junior officer, was in the hanger bay talking with divisional personnel. Fighter jets were stacked in the bay. Suddenly, a white dove flew into the bay and landed on a parked fighter jet aircraft. It was a confused white dove unable to find an exit to freedom. I directed the men to capture the bird and release it to the wild from which it came. The men were in the process of capturing the bird when a senior LTCMDR came along and countermanded my directive. He told them to capture and kill the bird, which he claimed was obviously diseased and could hold hazards to the navy. The LTCMDR and I held little regard for each other, but I never suspected he would be so short-sighted and would hold so little regard to a symbol of peace. To little avail, I suggested he was making a mistake. The men captured and killed the lovely symbol of peace. While many questioned our actions in Vietnam, we were publicly quiet concerning our views. Killing the symbol of peace convinced me we were making grave mistakes in Vietnam.

VOLCANO KRAKATOA

WE were passing through the Sunda Straits on our way to the Philippines, and I was on the bridge with the captain and the other bridge officers. As we looked to the left, we could see the famous Volcano Krakatoa which erupted in the 1800s and caused Vermont and other areas to have no summer. As we looked left, the captain said, "You could crack a toe over there!"

FIRST SUSHI

I was just a Vermont farm boy new to the sites of Japan and its food. My friend suggested we step inside a sushi bar and order some food. Our preferred food in Vermont was a venison steak. It was my very first experience with raw fish, and the plate had a green item that looked like a mashed vegetable. I forked the green stuff into my mouth and had an immediate burning sensation which a lot of Japanese beer helped quench. I was then told that it was an item called wasabi to accompany the fish as a sauce.

PUTTING OUT A FIRE ON AN AIRCRAFT CARRIER

I qualified as an Officer of the Deck (OOD) after several months on the U.S.S. *America*. The OOD serves at the pleasure of the captain and oversees the ship when the captain is not present on the bridge. With the captain present on the bridge, the OOD serves as the captain's assistant and directs the activities of the ship (not the air wing). During air operations, it is necessary to calculate a heading to provide proper wind speed for aircraft operations. Emergencies or near emergencies are always present on a carrier with 5,000 men. On average, a fire occurs every day on a carrier. Fortunately, most of those fires are minor and quickly extinguished. On this day, I was the OOD, and a fire broke out in one of the steam catapults. If the ship is turned in a direction which causes the wind to blow across the catapults, a fire can be extinguished. On this day, the Navigator Commander recommended a wind speed and direction to the captain. The captain turned to me and requested my advice on wind speed and direction. I gave my recommendation which was different from the navigator's.

I had become accustomed to quickly calculating speed and direction changes and felt quite comfortable with my recommendation. The captain told me to enact my recommendation and as I did so, the fire went out. I felt uneasy because the commander was senior to me and was a likeable fellow who I had made to look bad in front of the captain.

SIR, I'M GOING TO DEFLECT

AFTER one of our line periods off the coast of North Vietnam, we cruised to Japan for some much-needed rest. We were warned about those who wanted to defect and often used Japan as a gateway to Sweden and other countries. I was Officer of the Deck in Port late one evening when the chief on the after deck warned me about an out of control enlisted man. He came aboard drunk and informed the chief he was going to defect. I called the Marine guards to be on the lookout for an enlisted man out of control. A few moments later, an enlisted man came running up the hanger bay yelling, "Sir, I'm going to deflect." I, along with the Marines, approached him, and I told him he could do all the deflecting he wanted while he dried out downstairs in a holding cell. However, I said he could not defect, and probably tomorrow he would not remember a thing!

THOSE BOZOS WON'T MAKE IT

I was in Boston in 1967 for my physical for Navy OCS. I stayed overnight and decided to attend one of the Boston Red Sox games at Fenway. The Sox struggled through the game, and halfway through I left and said to myself "These bozos will never make it this year." They did make it and provided me and some others in my situation some relief. I was at OCS in Newport, Rhode Island, and we were up at 5:00 a.m. and asleep by 10:00 p.m. The Red Sox were playing in the series, and our tactics instructor was a red-haired Irish lieutenant from Boston... a true Red Sox fan. When the Sox were playing in the series, he would turn on the projector, show us victory at sea movies, and listen to the series downstairs. It was our chance to catch some sleep during the movies... the only thing missing was the popcorn.

POST FORESTALL FIRE

ONE of the many tragedies in the Vietnam War was a fire aboard the U.S.S. *Forestall*, a carrier operating in the South China Sea in 1967 and 1968. The fire caused many deaths and injuries aboard the carrier. Following the fire, further safety measures were instituted for carriers operating in the South China Sea. I served as one of the safety officers on one of the aircraft elevators during at sea transfer of weapons. The captain would make an announcement on the PA system prior to the operation directing the men to follow safety guidelines and operate equipment in a safe manner. The men from my division were operating the forklifts moving the many weapons, and I would direct them to follow the captain's message concerning safety. Quietly, I would remind them should they cause a safety problem it would be their ass and not the captain's ass on the line. The captain would again utilize the PA system after the completion of the weapons transfer at sea. He would announce a certain elevator as a winner for moving the most amount of ammunition on board during the shortest time. My elevator never won the award for movement of ammunition aboard. The captain provided two different messages for the men.

PLANES LOST IN VIETNAM

IT was the U.S.S. *America's* first Vietnam tour and we lost a plane and pilot a week to the forests and jungles of Vietnam. Commander Wilbur, the commander of an air wing who flew an F4, was our first loss. He was a devout officer who conducted religious services on the way to the conflict zone. He was captured by the North Vietnamese and placed in the Hanoi Hilton. After God knows how much torture, he condemned the war and thereafter was labeled as a turncoat by the navy and his fellow officers. He fought in Korea and come of age in World War II. Vietnam was a different war and viewed differently by many junior officers aboard the carrier. I am convinced his words came from his convictions and soul searching while a prisoner. He became convinced it was the wrong war, at the wrong time, for the wrong reasons.

BULLPUPS AND SIDEWINDERS

ALTHOUGH I was trained in nuclear weapons, I became the Air Missile Officer on the U.S.S. *America*. The aircraft carried two air-to-air missiles during combat missions over North Vietnam. The Sidewinder, a Korean War heat seeker and the Bullpup, a later radar-controlled missile. The pilots had good luck with the Sidewinder, but the Bullpup often failed. Finally, the company responsible for the missile sent a series of experts to the carrier to determine the problem. I don't know if it were successfully corrected before the next cruise as I left the ship.

CURTIS LEMAY

GENERAL Curtis Lemay, the man responsible for much of the firebombing over Japan and the man who wanted Kennedy to take a more aggressive stand during the Cuban Missile Crisis, was a vice presidential candidate. He was running as vice president with Presidential candidate George Wallace. General LeMay was visiting Vietnam and scheduled a couple of days aboard the U.S.S. *America* while we were off the coast of North Vietnam performing air operations. I finished a bridge watch and was stepping onto the flight deck as his C2 landed and taxied toward the bridge area. I watched as Secret Service agents departed the airplane with their machine guns drawn, followed by the general. I was amused, since we were off the coast on a carrier with no threat to the general. Of course, as a person infamous for some of his actions, he was not taking any chances.

ABSENTEE BALLOT

WHILE in Vietnam I mailed the town clerk in Brookline, Vt and requested an absentee ballot. I am not sure she knew what an absentee ballot was or where to obtain one. If she did, she did not send me one. I suspect she thought I would vote Democratic and did not send me my vote. I was denied the opportunity to vote while in Vietnam defending our democracy.

MANAGEMENT TRAINING

YOU spend ninety days in officer training and are then commissioned and assigned to a unit. They say you are an officer and a gentlemen and expected to manage people. It is the first management opportunity for most and often a rude awakening to the realities of dealing with people. I assumed command of a division without any previous management experience. Many of the men were either my age or older, and some witnessed combat during World War II and the Korean conflict. During the first week, my World War II divisional chief introduced himself in a very diplomatic manner. He would manage the daily activities of the division and keep me informed, an arrangement which provided for a good working relationship. I was pleased with his suggestion and learned much from an experienced chief. Complaints from the men concerning the chief's punishment went unanswered from me. I backed the chief, and he backed me. The division ran well, and I was well informed on all divisional issues, even those that needed no action on my part. The chief taught the importance of experienced personnel and delegation. A commission was no substitute for experience. Unfortunately, few of the ninety-day wonders were quick learners and suffered the consequences.

TAKING A NAVY SHOWER

THE carrier made its own potable water while at sea. Enlisted men were required to take navy showers. Navy showers consisted of wetting your body, turning off the water, soaping yourself, and then rinsing the water off, thus saving water. A young man in my division refused to bath and started stinking. Several men approached me and complained about the smell in their close living areas. They sought my advice on handling the situation. I said it would be inappropriate to provide advice to solve the problem. However, were I them I would know how to handle the problem without asking an officer. If I heard about their actions, my ears would be closed. They gave the man a navy shower… a gang scrub down. After the scrub down, the man became fond of showers and water. One day while taking more than a navy shower, he was written up by a first-class petty officer. He was sent to a captain's mast, or a judiciary hearing before the captain of the ship. As the divisional officer, I was in charge of defending the man. I informed the captain about the man's historic lack of showering and utilizing the ship's waters. I calculated the man was only using his reserve water and therefore was not in violation of the ship's policies. The captain dismissed the charges.

ASSIGNING A PERSON TO THE LAUNDRY

THE ship's laundry was a hot and unsettling place to work. My division was required to send a man to work in the laundry every three months. Since we dealt with weapons, we were keen on keeping the most experienced and capable men in the division. Those less capable were selected for laundry duty. I received a call from the laundry asking me to send another man to the laundry. I told them I would do so as soon as the man I sent returned. They told me he never showed up three months ago. I asked them why we were not told, and they did not reply. We were in port for retrofits, and I checked the pay records. The man in question was showing up for his pay every two weeks. Unfortunately, the word was out, and he did not show for his next pay. However, the shore patrol eventually found him, and he faced the captain's mast. The man was mentally incapable of planning his ruse. The captain asked him for information on those who had helped him. The man refused and was sent to the Marine's lockup on the ship. He was to be held there until he agreed to divulge his accomplices. At about 3:00 a.m. the next morning, I received a call from the Marines telling me the man wanted to see me and was ready to talk. I went down to the lockup and found the man with swollen eyes and other bruises. He said he wanted out and would tell all, which he did!

HOW TO RUN A NAVY

TODAY Brazil is a strong economic country with an abundance of agricultural and industrial products. It is one of the more robust South American countries. My carrier visited Rio on the way to Vietnam and again on the return from the conflict zone. Brazilian Navy officers were flown onto the carrier a week before our second arrival in Rio. They spent a week learning about our carrier operations. At that time, the Brazilians owned a World War II British carrier and a World War II American submarine. The carrier could not conduct flight operations because there was no Brazilian Naval Air Force, and the Brazilian Navy and Air Force had a poisonous relationship. The sub leaked and could not submerge. Thus, the Brazilian services were no match for our one carrier.

DISPLINARY ACTION

MOST of the senior officers on our aircraft carrier were World War II and Korean War veterans. Unfortunately, they viewed the Vietnam conflict differently than the 1960's officers like me. We were more than respectful to most of those veterans. However, there were a few full of themselves. I remember a friend telling one of those officers to go "fuck himself." The officer responded he would seek was disciplinary action. My friend responded, "What are you going to do, send me to Vietnam?"

WON'T BE AS BAD AS THEY SAY IN ICELAND

ONE of my fellow junior officers who arrived aboard with me found it difficult to comply with the navy dress requirements. His uniforms were always wrinkled, his shoes dirty, and he refused to have haircuts. The navy labeled him a non-conformist and sent him to Iceland. Before he left, he told me "it couldn't be as bad as it was rumored." A couple of months after he left, I received a postcard from him and he wrote, "It is worse."

THREATENED BY THE RED CHINESE

IN 1968, the US had yet to establish relations with Communist China. We were not allowed to visit China. I have pictures of my friends and I standing at a point at which we could not go beyond. Everything purchased in Hong Kong was to have a certificate indicating it was not produced or purchased in red China. It was a fallacy because many of the goods were obviously from the other side of the border. When we left the Hong Kong Harbor, we passed within a mile or two of the Chinese shore. I was on the bridge when we received a message from shore directing us to leave Chinese waters. They indicated they would fire upon us were we to neglect their warnings. I think the captain replied to the effect, "Go to hell." We could not imagine starting a new world war with a weak China.

MOONLIGHT IN VERMONT - CARAVAN EAST

THE Caravan East was a famous country and western watering hole in Albuquerque. Famous country and western groups played there… "Fats and Scruggs," "Glenn Campbell," etc. All of us at the nuclear weapons training would go there and drink until closing and then get up early the next day. One evening, a famous group was playing, and I asked them to play "Moonlight in Vermont." They did so, but more with a western beat.

ALMOST DROWNING IN HONG KONG HARBOR

THE U.S.S. *America* was anchored in the middle of the Hong Kong Harbor. We were ferried to shore in a small craft stored in our hanger bay. Due to the approach of a typhoon, all personnel were ordered back to the ship. Typhoons can be dangerous to shipping, and the U.S.S. *America* would be departing Hong Kong earlier than planned.

Many of us were taking the last craft toward the carrier when the harbor started surging from the storm. Passengers started to panic as the wave washed into the craft. They stood up forcing the center of gravity of the craft to shift… thus, forcing more water into the craft. As the water started to pour in, I could only think about my swimming abilities and the roughness of the harbor. My friend, a senior lieutenant, saved the day. He ordered everyone to lie down in the center of the boat and thus lower the center of gravity. Although we were all soaked, the craft arrived safely at the side of the carrier.

DO YOU SPEAK WITH AUTHORITY?

WE were due to leave on a second Vietnam tour aboard the *America* when the navy started decommissioning ships and downsizing its force. They gave us three options: we could leave within thirty days, stay our normal tour, or make a career in the navy. I think over ninety percent chose the first option as no one looked forward to another Vietnam tour. I was recently married, and my decision was easy. We were released into the inactive reserves, and most of us totally forgot our navy connections. I attended graduate school and one day received a letter directing me to the nearest Naval Reserve Center for a physical. The physical would allow for my advancement to the rank of lieutenant. Since the navy was in my past, I discarded the letter. My friend in Pennsylvania received the same letter and disposed of it in a circular file. A few weeks later, we received a registered letter from the navy department signed by a woman captain (colonel). The letter ordered us to go to the nearest reserve center and receive our physical and stated that actions would be taken against us if we failed to do as directed. I did as ordered and several weeks later received my advancement to full lieutenant. My friend decided to call the center sending the orders.

He asked to speak to the person who signed the order. He politely told her that he did not care to be advanced to full lieutenant. She told him to do as ordered and failure to do so would result in disciplinary action. My friend asked if she spoke with authority. She was a captain, in charge of the unit and was being advanced to rear admiral. My friend told her to take the letter and shove it where the sun doesn't shine. My friend never received his discipline.

WEARING NAVY UNIFORM AT PARTY

MY wife and I operated a bed and breakfast in Essex, New York. It was a wonderful little community where we became good friends with a number of people. One New Year's Eve, one of the other bed and breakfast owners held a costume party. Since I had been in the navy, I ordered a navy uniform from a costume company in Boston. I was having fun socializing when an agitated gentleman walked up and told me it was against the law to impersonate a naval officer. I laughed and said I had impersonated a naval officer during the Vietnam conflict, and no one had challenged me!

BEND DOWN AND KISS YOUR ASS GOODBYE

AFTER my graduation from OCS as a navy ensign, I was sent to the Sandia Base in Albuquerque, New Mexico for nuclear weapons training. I was raised during the Cold War and remember the real possibility of a nuclear war during the Cuban Missile Crisis. I remember practicing hiding under our school desks for training during a nuclear explosion. I was a bit apprehensive about being trained in nuclear weapons. During our first day of class, the instructors introduced themselves as experts on nuclear devices. They were part of a quick response team, sent to any area with a nuclear device problem. On the first day of class, they passed out nuclear safety cards, which we were to carry at all times. The cards read: "In Case of a Nuclear Explosion, Bend Down, and Kiss Your Ass Goodbye!"

HOTSIE BATH IN JAPAN

BETWEEN one of our battle stations, we cruised to Japan and anchored in Yokohama. Many of us planned to travel to Tokyo and meet at the

Hilton where we would purchase a famous Japanese bath with Geisha girls. Tokyo seemed more like New York City, and another officer and I decided to travel toward Mount Fuji. Prior to leaving, we were told the Japanese word for a "Hotsie Bath" and set out on our way. We went to the train station and purchased tickets toward Mount Fuji. Other than going toward Fuji, we really did not know where we were going. During the first night, we stayed at a small Japanese hotel. I remember going to a Japanese restaurant where they did not understand English. Fortunately, they had displays of their menus in the window with the Japanese characters. The officer I traveled with was a very good artist, and he would copy the symbols and present it to the waitress. Wherever we went, we would go to bars and ask for the Hotsie bath. Often, the bartender would get mad and kick us out. We did not think we were ordering anything bad. Finally, we arrived at a small town next to Mount Fuji and had a wonderful time buying silk kimonos and Japanese art. On the way back, we stopped at the city with the big Buddha and went into a bar. Fortunately, the bartender spoke English, and she told us the word we had been given was the word for "House of Prostitution." The word was anathema to the Japanese... no wonder we were kicked out of bars and restaurants. She directed us to a nice hotel down the street run by an older Japanese couple. It was an older hotel, and before we could enter, we had to remove our shoes in the Japanese fashion. We told the couple, using our new word for bath, what we desired. I was led into a private bath, as was my friend. The older woman came into the bath and showed me how to start the water. I did so expecting any minute a nice young Japanese woman in a kimono would come in and rub me down. My friend on the other side of the wall expected the same. After some time when no one appeared to take care of washing me, I dressed and went to the front of the hotel. Shortly, my friend joined me. We tried to pay the Japanese couple, but they would take no money. To this day, I can hear them laughing as we walked up the street. We provided excitement and amusement to this elderly couple.

SNAKES IN PHILLIPINES

OLONGOPO was the city adjacent to the Subic Bay Naval Base. It is not difficult to imagine the city: monkey meat being sold in the streets and sex sold in the bars. Just about everything was for sale in the city. There was a small island off the base the navy used as a recreation area. It contained a small bar, a golf course, and other recreational facilities. The Japanese used the island during World War II, and several gun emplacements without the guns were still on the island. Several of us elected to explore the island. We went into the jungle and visited the many gun emplacements. We did not think about any dangers confronting us. When we returned to the ship, the navy newspaper contained an article about the island. The guns had been removed and sent to Washington state as a memorial. When they removed the guns, they faced difficulties with all the cobra snakes. I think we probably had one or two cobras' looking us in the eye as we visited the emplacements. It would have meant sure death to any of us bitten by a snake.

DRUNK AND BRIDGE WATCH

AFTER thirty-five or forty days at sea, it was not unusual for junior officers to spend time drinking. We went to the officer's club in Subic and ordered mixed drinks for thirty-five cents. One day, our ship was scheduled to leave Subic late in the evening. We had been drinking all day and were quite drunk by the time the ship departed. I was not qualified as OOD yet, but was a Junior OOD. The captain did not notice we were not functioning well since there was a good enlisted detail also on the bridge. When the captain left the bridge for the evening, the OOD asked the enlisted to wake us if there were any ships within five miles. We all fell asleep for a couple of hours until our watch was over. Somehow, the captain learned of what happened and threatened to nail everyone if it happened again.

POOR JOHNNY IS SICK AND CAN'T MAKE THE SHIP

WE were in port when one morning and I received a call from the mother of a young sailor assigned to my division. She informed me her son would not be at the ship because he was not feeling well. I told her not feeling well was not an excuse for not showing up. I said he had a duty to show up, and if he was not feeling well, he could go to the ship's infirmary. I said if he did not show up, I would be sending out the shore patrol to arrest him. She got the point and said. "Johnny will be in."

YOU TALK LIKE YOU HAVE SHIT IN YOUR MOUTH

AS a junior officer of the deck in training, my duties were to instruct the helmsman on the course to steer. New helmsmen were often appearing on the watch, and I would notice their accents when they repeated orders. It became a game to guess origins based on their accents. One day, a new recruit appeared as the helmsman, and when he repeated my order, I knew instantly where he came from. I said, "I recognize your accent because you talk like you have 'shit in your mouth.'" He had a sense of humor and laughed and said, "Yes, sir." I said, "You are from Burlington, Vermont." "Yes, sir," he replied, "I am from Burlington, Vermont."

CHAPTER 9

STATE GOVERNMENT

Vermont Legislature

<><><><><><><><><><><><><><><><><><><><><>

THE VERMONT LEGISLATIVE COUNCIL

MY first state government position was with the Vermont Legislative Council. I, along with five others, provided the Vermont General Assembly with legislative research, committee work, bill drafting, and other services. We were hired to provide non-partisan assistance to all 180 legislators. It was a wonderful time in Vermont. It was the 1970s and the time of the environmental movement and the back-to-the land movement. Legislators were fiscally prudent. Many had suffered through the Depression, and it left a mark on their fiscal actions. The legislature, although both Democratic and Republican, was functional and based on individual relationships rather than party partisanship. Most legislators stayed in Montpelier during the session and thus socialized together in the evenings. A name on proposed legislation was more important than party affiliation. My position allowed me to gain a wonderful understanding of the legislative process, state government, and the functioning of bureaucracies.

Beginning in September, members would start introducing their ideas for legislation. It was our responsibility to take their ideas, discuss them with the sponsors, and put them into legislative language. For instance, if a member asked for a bill to outlaw fox hunting in Vermont, we would put it into bill form in legislative language. Every request was not always drafted because sponsors might withdraw the request before the draft. Most ideas were followed up with a draft bill. We would usually sit down at the beginning of the week and sort out the requests. I would often receive requests related to energy, natural resources, and agriculture.

DO AS WE SAY AND YOU WILL BECOME A LEADER!

HARRY was a farm member of the legislator from Lyndon, Vermont. Like most farmers, he was fiercely independent and made up his own mind relative to issues. He took me aside one day and told me why he did not get ahead in the Republican-controlled legislature. He said when he arrived, he was told if he went to the Republican conference and voted on legislation as he was told he would move ahead. He went to his first conference and was told how to vote. When the vote came to the floor, he voted contrary to his instructions. It was a lesson on moving forward, and he loved his independence more than advancement!

CAN ONLY COUNT TO THIRTY

JIM was a lobbyist for the Vermont Truck and Bus Association. He looked like the Irishman he was and spent all his time in the Senate, which was composed of thirty members. I never once saw him in the house with its 150 members. One day, he asked me to lunch to discuss legislation, as I had assumed the position with the legislative council and was getting to know both the lobbyist and legislators. I asked him why he spent all his time in the Senate, never to be seen in the house. He gave me the obvious answer; there were fewer votes to count in the Senate.

HE IS STILL OUT TO LUNCH

REID served as the legislative sergeant of arms and kept members happy. He hired the doorkeepers and otherwise was responsible for the legislators and their needs. Ethel, a wonderful older woman, worked as his assistant. Reid would sometimes take longer than normal lunch breaks. He was known to attend free conference lunches held at the tavern. Well after lunch when Reid should be back at his desk, someone would call and ask for him. Rather than tell them he was busy and would call them back, she would say, "He's still out to lunch and has not come back."

WILL SOMEONE TURN ME ON!

REPRESENTATIVE C was from a small town near the Massachusetts border. She was a lovely woman and was not afraid to stand up and ask a question or make a point on a particular bill. Every representative sat at a desk and had a small microphone they could pick up and utilize when speaking. Some members did not need the microphone and were able to make their voices carry. She was not one of those persons. One day, she stood up and started to speak. Suddenly, she realized that the microphone in her hand was not working. She raised her voice and said, "Mr. Speaker, can someone turn me on." The chamber erupted in laughter.

THROWING WINE AT THE GUEST

I attended a national legislative conference in Albuquerque, New Mexico. It was 1972, and President Nixon was in the middle of Watergate, the famous break-in that led to his resignation. There were two or three senators and two or three legislators who attended the conference. Each carried a fifth of booze in our suitcases from the Vermont Liquor Commission. We were going to party with the booze. We all arrived safely, except for a representative from Ludlow who picked up his suitcase with booze dripping out. It was a conference where New Mexico spared no expense. At the reception, there were all kinds of New Mexican food as well as a fountain spilling out tequila drinks. The main dinner for the reception had a head table with the governor, the leaders of the two chambers, the national legislative conference leaders, and the speaker. The main speaker was a national syndicated columnist by the name of Kilpatrick. He was a conservative columnist who had backed Richard Nixon. On this particular night, he stood up and talked about the problems in Washington. He said he had believed Nixon was innocent and the Watergate mess was insufficient to cause his impeachment. However, he said he had changed his mind; Nixon had lied, and he thought he should resign. At that moment, a New Mexican state senator at the head table stood

MAKING POT ILLEGAL

IN 1972, when I was hired by the Vermont legislature to work for the legislative council they hired two people : a young lawyer with a Harvard law degree and me with a master's degree in Resource/Agricultural Economics. Pot or marijuana was legal in Vermont prior to 1973, and the public safety commissioner, through a representative, submitted a draft request to make smoking pot a crime. The young lawyer was awarded the request. Our offices were in the state house. My associate invited the colonel of the Vermont state police to visit him in the state house to discuss issues related to the drafted bill. The colonel came to the state house bedecked in his police uniform with all the official insignia. My associate started discussing the intricacies of outlawing the possession of pot. He calmly opened his desk drawer, took out a joint, and started to smoke. Unfortunately, the colonel lacked a sense of humor. My associate's state house tour was cut short, and he was relegated to areas where marijuana smoking was overlooked.

SALMON RESTORATION

GEORGE Aiken was retiring as Vermont's senior U.S. Senator. During the Vietnam War, he told President Johnson to "declare victory and get the hell out." Senator Aiken was giving his farewell address to a joint session of the Vermont legislature. Tom Salmon had been elected governor and introduced the senator to a standing ovation. Senator Aiken started by saying he had voted for the Salmon Restoration Act, but he didn't think Vermont would restore the first salmon.

ELEPHANT IN STATE HOUSE

REID Lefebvre was a legislator from Manchester, Vermont in the 1960s. He operated a traveling circus with elephants. One day he brought his elephant to the state house. Unfortunately, it was before my time, but my friend Al Moulton told me that he rode the elephant into the state house. What a sight it must have been with an elephant roaming the

THE STATE IS GOING TO BUY A RAILROAD

THE St. Johnsbury and Lamoille Railroad was a bridge line running from Swanton to St. Johnsbury, Vermont. The line was built at the turn of the century to connect Portland, Maine to the Great Lakes. The connection to the Great Lakes was never finished. The line connected two main lines: the Central Vermont line in Swanton, Vermont with the Maine Central line in St. Johnsbury. The tonnage on the line had declined and the tracks were in need of substantial repair. The owner of the line was looking for a buyer. One of the main commodities transported was feed and lumber - feed to a mill in St. Johnsbury and lumber to other markets. Due to the track conditions, accidents were occurring frequently, and in some places, trains could not travel more than five miles per hour. It would cost thousands to upgrade the line for commerce to pass at a decent speed. The Legislature appointed a special committee to study the feasibility of purchasing the line. Senator Fred Westphal from Lamoille County was selected as chairperson of the special committee. Senator Westphal was a wise older gentleman with an entrepreneurial spirit who loved railroads and was convinced the purchase was the correct decision for the state. I was selected to staff the special committee and work with the chairperson. He asked me to set up a ride on the St. Johnsbury and invite Major Davis from the Vermont state police, who was a railroad enthusiast. On the appointed day, we met in Swanton and started the five miles-per-hour ride on the railroad. The tracks were in terrible shape, and it was not uncommon to see spikes popping free from the tracks. Major Davis was a railroad buff and when not policing, spent much of his time around railroads. Major Davis told me when tracks spread, and the cars are separated it was called a "shit out" in railroad terms. I expected a "shit out" at any moment.

As a staff member of the committee, I was expected to write the final report. Business interests and St. Johnsbury companies came before the committee supporting the purchase as necessary for the continued health of St. Johnsbury. The animal feed processing company stated the railroad was necessary for the continuation of their business. Feed was one of the main products transported over the line. They would close without the railroad. Fred told me to write the committee report prior to the committee voting on the state purchase. I told him the committee had not yet considered the facts and voted. He said not to wait for any committee action. He told me to write a report with a recommendation for the purchase of the railroad. I did so, and the state did purchase the line and pour thousands into its upgrade. Shortly after the state purchased the line, the feed company announced that it was closing its plant in St. Johnsbury. The line eventually failed, and today parts of it serve

DON'T JUDGE A BOOK BY IT'S COVER

THE chairperson of the Natural Resources Committee was a farmer from a small town near Burlington. He was tall in statue and drove an old Checker's taxicab. He adjusted the seats so his tall frame could comfortably fit into the front seat. He always wore an older suit, and you would often see him wearing a well-used hat as he entered the chamber. I marveled at his intelligence and ability to lead his committee through the difficult challenges of adopting important and often landmark legislation. While I did not know of his wealth, I had heard rumors. When a new class of legislators joined the general assembly, one mentioned to me he did not think the hillside farmer was very intelligent. I quickly corrected his assessment. I told the new member he was probably the wisest and most intelligent member and perhaps, the richest, although I did not know the amount of his wealth or the source. Many years later, after the member had died, I was visiting with a lawyer who was the farmer's friend. He told me the Vermont estate tax on his estate at the time of his death was $40 million. He also told me a story about Alan Greenspan, the former Federal Reserve Chairperson placing conditions on an invitation to speak. He told the inviting group he would only speak if two of his best students were also invited: Warren Buffet and H, the former chairperson of the Natural Resources Committee and the hillside farmer.

PROFESSIONAL LICENSING
TO PROTECT THE PUBLIC

AS one of the junior members of the legislative council staff, I was assigned drafting requests related to professional licensing. The number of occupations seeking either changes in legislation or legislation to license their occupations was interesting. It was always framed with the interest of protecting the public. Of course, in most cases, it was in the interest of protecting the occupation. There are definite reasons to license certain occupations like medicine where a person can be injured, but the argument is less persuasive with other occupations. I remember representatives of the funeral directors once arguing for changes to protect the public. I kiddingly asked them how many clients complained! There were requests to license mechanics, carpenters, fishing guides, and a host of other professions.

WRITING AND IMPLEMENTING AGRICULTURAL DEVELOPMENT LEGISLATION

THE governor's food commission report was published recommending a series of actions to improve agriculture in Vermont. The Agricultural Agency in Vermont was primarily a regulatory agency with no marketing resources. I staffed the House and Senate Agricultural Committees which created legislation forming a marketing division in the Vermont agency as well as creating a seal of quality. Little did I realize I would be staffing the agency and assuming responsibility in the Agency. I worked creating the Agricultural Marketing Division and creating the first Vermont seal of quality.

HIS VOTE COULD BE PURCHASED WITH AN ICE CREAM CONE!

THE legislature changed the age when a person could become a member of the chamber. Prior to 1970, one had to be 21 before elected to the chamber. In 1971, they changed the age to a younger 18. At 18, the St. Johnsbury house member was the youngest person to ever serve in the House of Representatives. He was young and had an obvious chip on his shoulder. John C. was a successful lobbyist from Rutland who weekly took the young legislator out to lunch. We said his vote could be had for an ice cream cone. Unfortunately, he went on to greater fame by serving a prison sentence for killing a person in St. Johnsbury.

TRIP TO NIAGARA FALLS AND BEYOND

TOWARD the end of the legislative session, a time arrives when only the members on the appropriation committees are busy. This was downtime for other members of the assembly. Francis, a senator from Franklin County, decided to take a journey to Niagara Falls and asked Harlan, a house member friend from Enosburg Falls, to join him. Francis would drive and take care of all expenses. He normally carried a wad of cash in his pocket. They started for Niagara Falls and kept going until they reached San Francisco. They decided to see more of the country. The family was not sure where they were until a call was received requesting the wiring of money so they could return home.

DDT IS NOT HARMFUL!

WHEN Rachael Carson wrote *Silent Spring*, it was only a matter of time before DDT and like pesticides were outlawed. The damage done to birds and other wildlife was enormous. In the early 1970s, some of the legislative farmers remembered using DDT, and I am sure some still housed the chemical and perhaps still used it illegally. One of the senator farmers from Addison County said he used it regularly, and when he mixed it, he would taste it to see if it was the correct strength. I did note he was totally bald, had glasses, and walked bull legged.

GOVERNMENT RUN BY BANKER, BUSINESSMAN, FINANCIER

WE received many interesting drafting requests at the legislative council. One request by a new member immediately comes to mind. The legislator was a retired Montpelier banker concerned with the manner in which state government functioned. He thought state government would function efficiently if it was managed by a board consisting of a banker a business-man, and financial expert. I had no idea how to abridge a state constitu-tional problem. I spent some time thinking about the draft and even put pen to paper. My office was in the back of the state house with a drive-thru behind the state house. One day there was a rap on my window. The new member was holding a bag. I opened the window and he told me to forget the request. He thanked me and handed me a bag. Inside was a fifth of whiskey I shared with my fellow workers.

WHEN YOU SMELL FRAUD

I joined the legislative council in 1972 with a clear expectation Vermont politics was mostly clean and small. I grew up in the small town of Brookline, Vermont where all action was transparent and honest. There were few lobbyists and most legislators treated expenditures as if it were their own money. I saw few examples of legislation being introduced to benefit big money. I did notice a senator from Windsor County was always introducing legislation relating to horse racing. I did not put two and two together until I traveled to a legislative conference in Albuquerque, New Mexico. The senator was also in attendance and invited me to go to the horse races. He told me he was provided free tickets and some money for betting by some racing friends. I put two and two together and realized he supported racing bills in Vermont to further his own interests. Unfortunately, the same senator was later charged with absconding with client's money and lost his chance to become lieutenant governor of Vermont.

IF YOU WERE OLDER AND I WAS YOUNGER

OUR drafts of legislation were typed and sent to two semi-retired proof-readers. Alida Doe was a very attractive and bright 75-year-old who had acted in professional theatres. Helen Burbank served as Deputy Secretary of State when many of the heads of state departments were housed in the State House. Helen and Alida were about the same age. I found both very interesting and would spend time talking with them and kidding them about issues. I became friends with both and enjoyed listening to their historical perspective. One day, Alida announced if she was younger and I was older we would have one wonderful weekend together. Several years later after we both left the legislative council; I took a Christmas gift to her at her home on upper State Street. She aged considerably and had a slight stroke, but she was still sharp and ambulatory. As I left, she said, "I wish we could still have that weekend together."

WHY WOULD THE LEGISLATURE
NEED A COMPUTER?

IN 1972 when I joined the Vermont Legislative Council, there was a typing pool and all work was performed on IBM Selectric Typewriters. I suggested we try a computer and link it to the University of Vermont to help us with research. The Council provided me with a computer, and I tried to establish a phone connection with the University. We were unable to establish a secure network over which we could communicate with the library and researchers. It was the end of computers at the Vermont Legislature!

WHEY PLANT $100,000 QUESTION

THE Vermont legislature established the Vermont Whey Authority in 1969. The authority was created to eliminate the dumping of whey into Vermont's rivers and streams. Whey is the byproduct of cheese-making, and before the advent of the authority, it was customary to dump whey into the rivers and streams of Vermont. Whey as a by-product has a value as an ingredient in many products. The authority, with the bonding assistance and appropriation of the state, constructed a plant in Georgia, Vermont with the purpose of drying whey to sell on the commodity market. Whey suddenly had a value beyond its dumping in the streams and rivers. The authority hired a consultant charged with designing the Georgia, Vermont facility. The legislature was conducting a hearing due to costs over runs. I sat next to a legislative member and suggested he ask the $100,000 question. Where were the drawings for the proposed plant? The consultant replied and said everything was in his head.

THOUGHT CORNSTALKS WAS THE PASSWORD

KEITH was elected as representative for the Waterbury, Vermont district. Later, he became state senator for Washington County. Keith was a hill farmer with a few head of Jersey cows and often looked like he just left the barn. Keith served as president of the Vermont Farm Bureau. Looks can be deceiving, and Keith's looks certainly hid a sharp mind and quick wit. Keith graduated with a degree in forestry from Syracuse University. Keith and I became friends, and I was always awaiting his quick wit the house agriculture committee. He invited me to speak at a Grange meeting in Waterbury. I went to the door and knocked and a man came to the door. He asked me the password…I said "corn stalks". He said I should go and return when the meeting was finished as I did not know the password.

DON'T BUY THE RED CAR!

EVERY weekday morning, those of us who worked for the legislative council drafting legislation met for coffee in the cafeteria. We were often joined by legislators who became our friends. We were not a political arm and served both parties. Madeline Kunin and Jim Douglas, who both became governors, often joined our coffee group. Brian Burgess was a representative from Burlington, and he too became a regular attendee and friend. Brian ran for lieutenant governor and won. After he won, he was provided with a state car. He told us he was ordering a large red and comfortable vehicle. We advised him to rent a more muted vehicle as it would become an issue. Unfortunately, Brian ordered his red vehicle, and the press had a heyday.

I HAVEN'T SEEN ANY WILD TURKEYS

VERMONT had yet to establish a turkey season. Wild turkeys were introduced into Addison County and were quickly establishing themselves throughout the state. Prior to the 1800s when many of Vermont's forests were clear-cut, Vermont was home to the wild turkey. In 1974 a bill was introduced allowing wild turkey hunting in Vermont. Lieutenant Governor Jack Burgess presided over the Senate, and Senator Jack O'Brien from Winooski was one of its aged members. Senator O'Brien often fell asleep in his chair and after the session could be found sleeping on a bench upstairs with his pillow. The lieutenant governor announced the Senate had before them a bill relating to the hunting of wild turkeys in Vermont. Senator O'Brien suddenly shook himself awake and said he hadn't seen any wild turkeys in Vermont. The lieutenant governor replied, "Look in the mirror in the morning when you are shaving." Senator O'Brien responded, "But I don't drink and drive." The lieutenant governor had at least one drinking and driving experience which was noted in the press. So much for Senate decorum.

AGRICULTURAL DEPARTMENT MANAGEMENT

BRUCELLOSIS is a contagious cattle disease-causing cattle to abort prematurely. From 1974 to 1976, I served as deputy and acting commissioner of agriculture confronting the expanding disease problem in Vermont. In 1976, Ed Eurich was appointed commissioner, and I was retained as deputy commissioner. Under the scenario and plan put forth by Governor Snelling when he appointed Ed, I was to manage the department on a daily basis, and Ed was to serve as the public personality and represent the department in the legislature and at public events. Ed called me and asked to meet at the Holiday Inn in Waterbury. He asked me to stay on with the arrangement the Governor outlined. Of course, nothing happens as planned, and I don't neither of us expected the brucellosis outbreak to continue unabated. After several months, it was clear to me the governor's management experiment was not working for either me or Ed. It was unfortunate, for Ed was a wonderful man and our management approaches differed. I arranged for lunch with the governor's legal advisor and told him the arrangement was not working and I wished to leave. I said I would leave quietly, and perhaps, the governor could find another place for me in the administration. Bill reported the conversation to the governor, and Snelling invited me to his office. He told me I was to stay at the department, and if I left, he would inform the press of the problems in the department and the brucellosis outbreak was because of my mismanagement. I had no other choice but to remain in the department. Things did not improve either on the brucellosis front or between Ed and me. It did not take Dick long to order an investigation of the department. Ed was allowed to serve out his tenure, one of the vets was allowed to retire early, and I was moved to the energy office where I became Vermont's director of energy. I believe Snelling thought the energy office would be a quiet place where I could use my management skills to enhance new energy technologies and energy conservation. Things were about to change due to issues in the Mid-East.

ORGANIC FOODS IN THE 1970S

THE organic movement had its start as a contrary movement: hippies and non-conformists advancing their own concepts of growing without pesticides and other unnatural ingredients. In some ways, it harkened back to an earlier time when we used natural ingredients on our gardens and did not utilize pesticides, but in the 1960s and 1970s, it was more countercultural. My navy friend managed Walnut Acres, which was one of the largest organic farms. I was serving as acting commissioner of agriculture for Vermont, and Bob invited me to one of the first organic food shows. You would walk down the aisles, and someone might sprinkle white powder on you claiming it would "calm your nerves." There were legitimate products, but there was also what I would call far-out stuff. As the industry matured, it became less countercultural and more mainstream. Today, the likes of Whole Foods, Walmart, and other grocery chains carry varieties of organic and natural foods. The industry has accepted government regulations and oversight, becoming a multibillion-dollar industry.

NOT ENOUGH VODKA!

IN the late 1980s, Governor Kunin established a sister state relationship with one of the countries within the Soviet Union. She invited representatives of the country to Vermont. As secretary (commissioner) of agriculture, my agency was assigned responsibility for arranging their stays. My wife owned a bed and breakfast in Essex, New York overlooking Lake Champlain and held a party for the delegation. The governor of Vermont was in attendance as well as various Vermonters and members of the Essex community. There was a band, food, and much liquor. The delegation consumed as much vodka as we could purchase; we found it difficult to supply enough vodka for the delegation. They told us they did not have sufficient funds for their travel back to New York to board their plane. I provided an agency van and asked one of the employees to drive them to the plane. When he returned, he told me they asked him to stop at a well-known electronics store where they loaded up on electronic equipment to resell when they landed back in their home country. So much for not having sufficient funds to return home!

WHAT DID YOU DO IN VIETNAM?

SENATOR Bernie Sanders served as mayor of Burlington; Vermont was elected to Congress to replace Congressman Peter Smith. The new congressman made an appointment to come in and discuss dairy issues with me, the commissioner of agriculture. It was during the first invasion of Iraq under the first President Bush. I was opposed to the invasion and saw it as a move to protect our oil supply. I was wearing a pin, which said; "Keep the troops out of Iraq." Congressman Sanders sat down in my office and explained people suggested he visit with me because I was an expert on dairy policy. I thanked him and said I was not; there were many dairy policy experts. He sarcastically said he could see I was an expert on Iraq. It did ruffle my anger; so, I said, "Where were you in Vietnam?" Not that it really mattered for I never held it against anyone who did not serve. However, I did feel service gave you a different perspective on wars and fighting.

CONDOS ON HILLSIDE OF SKI AREAS

DEANE Davis served as Governor of Vermont and was the father of Act 250, which established environmental criteria for development in Vermont. Governor Davis traveled to Mount Snow, Vermont where he witnessed aggravated development causing serious environmental problems. As a conservative Republican, he saw the need to protect the environment in Vermont. After he retired, he was quoted as saying if he were to live longer, he would take an active part in making sure there were no condos on the ski area hillsides in Vermont. He recognized the soil and typography of the hillsides was not suitable for development.

YOU WORK FOR ME

WHEN you in government, it is not unusual to receive calls from outraged citizens. Citizens are angry when you make a decision contrary to their interests. A person would call and tell me since I was a public servant, I worked for them. As one of their employees, I was expected to act on their behalf. I told them 600,000 people populated Vermont and perhaps 599,999 wanted me to act contrary to their interest. I worked for all the citizens of Vermont. They should consider my actions in that light.

BRUCELLOSIS FROM DRINKING RAW MILK

WE drank raw milk on our dairy farm. We did not think about milk as a vector for diseases and grew to love the taste of raw milk. My grandfather placed the ten-gallon cans of collected milk in the water cooler on the farm where they would sit until picked up by the milk truck driver. On very hot days, we would sneak into the milk house and help ourselves to cold milk. When I first joined the Agricultural Department, the State was struggling with an outbreak of brucellosis on several farms. People drinking milk from infected cattle can develop undulant fever similar to a bout of the flu. I certainly was sick as a youth, but never connected it to the raw milk. The department field personnel collected blood samples from the infected herds to determine which animals were infected and were to be sent to slaughter. I asked them to take a sample of my blood to determine if I had the disease. The sample was positive indicating I had undulant fever as a child. I was now immune to the disease and could safely drink raw milk. Later, a large dairy farm in the Burlington area was selling raw milk, and some of their customers became sick. The Department introduced legislation to outlaw the sale of raw milk.

ICRAP

I was often amused by acronyms. Governor Snelling appointed me as Chair of the Interagency Committee on Rules and Administrative Procedures. Our purpose was to review the various agency rules before they were published. I found it amusing that it was represented by ICRAAP.

INVESTIGATING POSSIBLE MAFIA INVOLVEMENT

I was serving as Vermont's acting commissioner of agriculture. A Canadian Mozzarella company announced they would build a cheese plant in Vermont. There were accusations in the press the company was linked to the mafia. At one of his press conferences, Governor Snelling was asked about the company and its alleged links to the mafia. I was driving home and had the radio turned to a Waterbury, Vermont station reporting the news. They reported Governor Snelling was going to investigate the reported ties to the mafia, and he was going to appoint Ronald Allbee as his investigator. I quickly went to visit my neighbor who was with the FBI in Vermont. Al said that any company dealing in Mozzerala needed connections, but it did not mean they were necessarily Mafia. I performed a quick study and withdrew myself from the issue.

CALLING CHANNEL 3 NEWS IN BURLINGTON

ONE of the unfortunate responsibilities of being Commissioner of Agriculture was making decisions negatively affecting people. I voted against providing a loan to a farmer who was heavily in debt. He was angry and was forever my enemy. He called my office after the vote and told my secretary if I did not call him by 12:00 p.m. he would call Channel 3 news in Burlington and criticize me on air. I am not one to take threats seriously, and when someone lays down the gauntlet, it just causes me to react. About 15 minutes before 12:00 p.m., I called him and gave him the number for Channel 3. He did go on the news and criticize me for being part of the group which turned down his request for a loan.

INVESTIGATION OF A CHICKEN FARM INSPECTOR

THE Agency of Agriculture (Department of Agriculture) supplied inspectors for the Hardwick Chicken Operation owned by Leopold. One can imagine the working conditions in a chicken farm and the tenuous nature of the inspector's work as he looked at eggs coming off the line. It was not a comfortable work environment. The department supplied the inspectors and carried out the work of the USDA inspection unit. Leopold was always calling the chief of markets complaining about the inspections or the inspector. I met Leopold on many occasions and enjoyed talking with him and understood the difficulties of operating a business in Hardwick employing many who needed employment. One day, the chief of markets came into my office and said the Leopold called and said the inspector had used "foul" language in front of employees. Leopold wanted to know what the department was going to do about the actions of the inspector. I knew there were two sides to every story and asked the chief to ask Leopold if we could come up and talk to the employees involved. The chief and I traveled to Hardwick. We visited with Leopold who told us what the inspector said and was agitated. He directed us to the employees at the "breaking plant" up the road. The breaking plant was in a separate building and was the facility in which cracked eggs were broken into a large steel bowl to be sent to baking companies. I walked into the breaking plant, and several large Hardwick women were sitting around a large metal bowl breaking eggs. I introduced myself and said I was there to determine if the inspector used foul language in front of them. As soon as I stopped, one of the women said, "You bet your sweet ass the son of a bitch swore in front of us." I thanked them for their time, returned to Leopold, and told him the case was closed. I cautioned the inspector about his language in front of the women who might be cursing him.

HOW TO BE CONFIRMED

GOVERNOR Kunin announced my appointment as her secretary (commissioner) of agriculture. In order to assume the position, I had to be confirmed by the Vermont Senate. The Senate Committee scheduled a date, and I appeared in the committee room on the appointed time . I knew all the senators on the committee. When a quorum arrived, the chairperson announced the purpose of the hearing. He said they were there to confirm my appointment by the governor. He said they all knew me, and he did not think any hearing was in order. If they all agreed, they would move on to other business. I said I would be more than happy to answer any questions. No, they said, it would not be necessary. They moved on to other business after telling a few Vermont stories.

BACK DOOR TO AGRICULTURAL DEPARTMENT

WHEN I joined the Agricultural Agency in 1975, the back entrance was blocked by a wooden door with no lock. There was a robbery within the agency leading me to request for better replacement for the door. I asked for a steel door that could lock. I informed agency personnel that anyone who needed to enter after hours would be given a key. You would have thought I was taking away their long-lost child. They were really angry with me for taking away their long-loved door. Providing them with a key did not quiet their anger. They knew I was upset by their response, and at the annual Christmas party, they gave me the old door wrapped in holiday wrapping paper.

THE BOOTS ARE IN THERE, FIND THEM

THE Department of Agriculture provided dairy and meat inspector's boots. When the old boots were wearing out, they would purchase new boots and put the cost on their expense accounts. Our department budget manager was quite strict and denied the inspector's request for reimbursement. The inspector submitted another expense report the following month with a note attached, "The boots are in here, find them." His expenses included the boots within the expenses for travel, and the budget person could not challenge his travel expenses.

JUST MAKE THE PRIVATE SECTOR COMPLY

THE Vermont Pesticide Advisory Board made recommendations to the commissioner (secretary of agriculture). Private utilities spraying right of ways were required to submit a comprehensive environmental plan prior to a granting of a permit. Governor Kunin was very pro-environment and endorsed such requirements. The Transportation Agency was spraying right of ways without going through the same process. I required the agency to submit a plan under the same guidelines required of private groups. I received pushback from officials in the Transportation Agency, including the secretary. They informed me it was the first time such a requirement was placed on the agency and I was being difficult. The secretary informed me she would take the issue to the governor and I would see my decision overturned. I told her she was welcome to talk to the governor, but I still would not change my mind. I reminded the secretary the governor proudly supported such requirements for private groups, and I could not imagine her not supporting the same requirements for government agencies. The Transportation Agency did go through the process and I made some enemies in the agency.

WHAT IF THE IF PILGRIMS HAD LANDED ON SEAL ROCK!

THE U.S. Senate Committee, which Senator Leahy chaired, held a hearing in Montpelier, Vermont while I was Commissioner of Agriculture. All the members of the committee as well as the secretary of agriculture attended the hearings out of courtesy to the chairman. I was asked to raise money for gifts and a luncheon at the Shelburne Farms Inn overlooking Lake Champlain. The hearing was held at the state house in Montpelier, Vermont. I welcomed the senators to Vermont and moderated the hearing. Dick Lyng, a California farmer, was Secretary of agriculture. Dick was a very reserved, cultured, and kind gentleman. As a joke, he said if the Pilgrims had landed on "Seal Rock" instead of "Plymouth Rock," there would not be any agriculture in New England!

YOU DON'T DESERVE A BONUS

GOVERNOR Kunin asked me to prepare a work plan for the year. It was the plan upon which she measured my performance. I would work with the legislature creating such programs as the Agricultural Finance Program, increases in property tax abatement, increases in the promotional program, a regional dairy pricing program, and a one-time payment to each dairy farmer in Vermont. By any measure, it was an extraordinary year. We were so successful helping the farm community the chairperson of the education board asked me to stop helping farmers as it was drawing attention and money away from education. At the end of the year, the governor announced she was paying bonus dollars to four or five of her appointees. It became public information and was in the papers and other news media. I called my mother and asked if she had heard the news. She asked why I received a bonus as it was her tax dollars. She told me I was hired to do a job and should not expect a bonus. In my mother's world, you worked hard at your job and did not expect any other considerations. I said I received it because the governor thought that I had performed well. I also told her she would not receive a holiday present if she really thought I did not deserve a bonus. She received a holiday gift.

EMPLOYEES WILL RUN THE AGENCIES AND DEPARTMENTS

BEFORE Bernie Sanders successfully ran for Mayor of Burlington, he was running for governor of Vermont as a Liberty Union candidate. I was Acting Commissioner of Agriculture with an office directly across from the state house. It was noontime, and Bernie was on the state house lawn campaigning. Several state employees, some of whom I recognized as agency of agriculture employees, surrounded him. I ventured across the street to hear what Bernie was telling the group. As I neared, I heard him tell the employees if he were elected governor of Vermont, the employees and not the commissioners or secretaries would run the departments and agencies. I wanted to walk up to Bernie and tell him, "They already do."

NO MARSHALL PLAN FOR EUROPE

AS Vermont commissioner of agriculture, I was a proud recipient of a European community fellowship. I was allowed to choose three countries to visit as well as Brussels. The itinerary and expenses were arranged and paid for by the EUC. I choose Britain, France, and Holland. I was accompanied by their state department in every country and allowed to visit government ministers and other officials. I asked every official if Europe would support a Marshall-type plan for the rest of the world. To a person, they stated they would never support such a plan. I reminded them the U.S. helped restore Europe with the Marshall Plan. They thanked us but said it was not in their DNA.

DUKAKIS WILL LOOSE

GOVERNOR Kunin sent me and several other officials to Kennedy School of Government in Harvard for six weeks of study. Governor Dukakis was running for president against George Herbert Walker Bush and had a substantial lead in the polls. One of our professors at the school who taught press relations had worked for Dukakis. We asked if he thought Dukakis would win since he was well ahead. He told us he thought Dukakis would lose because he was not good at taking advice. He lost the election, and there is a famous picture of him with his head hanging out of a tank.

IT WOULD BE A RISKY INVESTMENT

VERMONT had several thousand dairy farms and many dairy cooperatives in the 1970's. The cooperative meetings were large and held often at various locations. During some of the cooperative meetings, two young hippies would market their wares and provide free daiquiris to the attending farm leaders. They were a fledgling company operated by individuals who had never been in business but were wonders at marketing They were looking for investors and actively marketing their products. In fact, on some Friday afternoons, they would go through the state office buildings in Montpelier and pass out free ice cream. I remember their daiquiris were popular, and people would line up to taste the ice cream with liquor. One of the cooperatives, St. Albans cooperative in St. Albans, Vermont was offered an opportunity to invest in the new ice cream company. The cooperative declined because they thought it was too risky an investment. Who would have thought what was considered to be a risky venture proved to be a very successful Ben and Jerry's, which would build the world's biggest ice cream sundae on the St. Albans common in the late 1970s? Cooperatives tend to be conservative, and I often wonder how things might have changed for the cooperative with the investment.

NATIONAL GOVERNOR ASSOCIATION MEETINGS

GOVERNORS belong to the National Governor's Association and attend the meetings. They like to rub shoulders with other governors, and in Kunin's case, she was rubbing shoulders with a governor from Arkansas named Clinton. She served on the Agricultural and Environmental Committee of the NGA and invited me to the meetings. When meetings were held in attractive spots like Chicago or Cincinnati, I would attend. I would try to send my deputy to less attractive locations. The committees were boring events where the staff hammered out NGA positions. Congress cared less what the NGA did; they listened to the voters. On one occasion, when attending the Washington meeting, I invited Senator Leahy's press aide to the hotel holding the event for some drinks. I preferred to sit at the bar rather than in the boring committee. Joe said when he worked for Governor Salmon and attended the committee meetings, Salmon once was mad at his staff. His staff left the meeting for an off-site bar. Salmon was not mad because they left, but because they did not tell him where they were so he could join them! Joe and were drinking at the bar when the governor's aide approached and said the governor asked for me. I wobbled in and sat as far away as possible, so she did not notice I was drunk!

WHERE ARE THE CAMERAS

I would represent Vermont at meetings of the commissioners of agriculture from the various states. I shall never forget one such meeting held in Virginia and hosted by my counterpart. The Virginia Department of Agriculture picked me up at the airport and drove me to the conference center. I exited the plane and found a person holding a sign with my name. We went to gather my luggage and he directed another gentleman with a tuxedo to pick up the luggage. The luggage was retrieved, and we started toward a car. There was a white limousine waiting for me. I asked if there were any cameras around as I did not want the governor to see me getting into a white limo. I was the only one in the limo, and I was deposited in style at the conference center. What a conference it was... we toured Jefferson's estate and spent a day at Kluge's estate a few miles from Jefferson's. John Kluge made his money in multi-media and owned the lavish estate in Virginia. The estate housed horses living in style in horse barns the envy of any horse owner. It made me want to be a Kluge horse. We were fed in style and entertained by a celebrity entertainer at his conference center. John Kluge and his wife were separated, and Ms. Kluge was going with the governor. In the evening, a very nice dinner was served under a tent. At the next table sat the Governor and Ms. Kluge, Armand Hammer and his nurse, and the senior Albert Gore and his wife.

DEALING WITH THE PRESS

ONE of the courses at the Kennedy School of Government covered dealing with the press. Most of the students in the class had a history of press dealings. The professor asked the students to discuss some of their press experiences. One student, a vice president of the Long Island Railroad, discussed his experiences. He said there had been a very difficult union boycott, and the press called to ask how he was dealing with the situation.

He said he felt like a bear with its ass hanging out of a cave! Unfortunately, the *New York Times* printed his response.

CHINESE RESTURANT IN BOSTON

ON one of my trips to Boston, my daughter Elizabeth, who was twelve, traveled with me. A Vermont friend who attended Harvard directed me to the best Chinese restaurant in Boston. The restaurant was in Chinatown and was located inconspicuously below the sidewalk. Liz and I both ordered a Chinese dish. Not long after ordering, a dish was placed in front of her and she took a few bites before realizing it was not the dish she ordered. Suddenly, the waiter grabbed the dish from the table, walked through the swinging doors, did a U-turn, and delivered the dish to another table. Fortunately, the other table did not see Liz eating their dish.

THEY WON'T REMEMBER WHAT WAS SAID!

WHEN Senator Leahy assumed the position of chairperson of the U.S. Senate Agricultural Committee, he promised to bring the committee to Vermont. I was serving as commissioner of agriculture at the time, and Leahy's staff asked me to help with the arrangements and raise the money to cover the costs. Enough money was raised to allow for a nice lunch on the Lake at Shelburne Farms. Hearings were held in Burlington and in Montpelier at the state house. I asked my staff to collect Vermont food products for a gift basket. They obtained a ten-pound cheese wheel box and filled it to the brim with Vermont products. The boxes were so large we had to deliver them to the plane parked at the air guard base in Burlington. I presented a box to each senator and the agricultural secretary as they were boarding the plane to return to Washington. Afterward, I received some grief from employees of the Agricultural Agency in Vermont for showering the visiting dignitaries with gifts. I told them the guests would hardly remember what they ate for lunch at Shelburne Farms, they certainly would not remember what was said at the hearings, but they would never forget the gifts they received upon leaving Vermont!

WHICH IS REAL HORSE'S ASS?

ONE of the luxuries of being commissioner of agriculture was the ability to meet farmers and rural residents of Vermont. As often as possible, I would tour different parts of the state and different farming areas. Horses were a growing industry in Vermont, and I decided to tour Benson, Vermont. Many old dairy farms in Benson had been converted into horse farms. A Rutland Hearld reporter writing a story about Benson accompanied me on the tour. As the tour was winding down, the reporter asked if she could take a picture of me with a horse. I told her on one condition: she had to take a picture of me with the horse's ass so the public would know who the real horse's ass was!

NO RESERVED PARKING SPACES

GOVERNOR Kunin, per her directive, directed appointees not to have their own parking spaces. It created difficulty when the legislature was in town and you were called to out-of-town meetings. I believe the governor felt we should suffer like others looking for parking spaces, even though it was an inconvenience. I noticed that the director of the highway board had a reserved parking sign on a building. I called my friend, the buildings and grounds commissioner and asked why. He said I could have a parking sign if I so desired. I thanked him and said it would create problems with Department personnel. I asked him to place a sign on the building which said, Reserved Agricultural Department, Shipping and Receiving. I said it would be my parking space. The governor had her own parking space!

PREPARATION H FOR MOSQUITO CONTROL

DURING one summer in the late 1980s it rained constantly and the mosquito outbreak in the Lake Dunmore area of Addison County became newsworthy. A newsman from one of the major national channels had relatives in the area, and he made it a national headline. Vermont had no active control program, and the district responsible had not completely been activated. Unfortunately, overall mosquito control fell within the Agricultural Department, and I had to deal with the nightly and weekly news. The governor was asked to commit money to the district, but she delayed. Thus, she became the focus of much of the news. They even made mosquito traps with the governor's name on them. At a meeting held in Addison County, I sent my deputy because he lived in the area. I told him beforehand that one of the questions he would be asked would be, "Is the Governor going to commit funds to the district to fight mosquitos?" I told him he was to say she was considering and not decided on the level of funding . Unfortunately, when asked the question, my deputy responded by saying he did not know what the governor was going to do. It became headlines and the governor called me over and asked me to fire the deputy. I put him on warning and give him a good dressing down. The headlines grew greater, and the governor was interviewed by the national news. She said if anyone had a solution to the mosquito problem, they were to write her. One of her first suggestions was to use "Preparation H" as an application. As we all know, it is used elsewhere on the body where the mosquitos do not venture.

THE MARKET WILL BE THE FINAL JUDGE!

BST or BgH is a naturally hormone in milk affecting the lactation of cattle. Monsanto, working with Cornell and other universities, developed a genetically modified BST or BgH which, when injected in the bovine, increased the lactation. It was the first genetically engineered product waiting approval from FDA. The public was divided on the acceptance of the product, and Monsanto had poured money in promoting the product with farmers. Dairy farmers were excited because it allowed them to increase their production. It became a politically hot potato, and Governor Kunin and I came out against utilizing an engineered product in a consumable good. The Commissioner of the Massachusetts Department of Agriculture, referred to the product as "Crack for Cows." Quite a catchy phrase. Our position made us unpopular with many in the dairy industry. We were troubled with the revolving door of scientists, the FDA's lack of transparency and their total neglect of the effect on the animals. I was also concerned the land grant college system charged with improving the economics of the farm family would purse technology likely to put farm families out of business. Vermont passed legislation requiring the labeling of BST products and also required those farms part of the trials be identified. I was asked to speak at a New England dairy promotional meeting of farmers. They were not happy as I explained our position, but I told them even if the FDA approved the material it would ultimately be the consumer approving or disapproving of the genetically engineered item. It turned out the consumer ruled against BgH and farmers found it was not beneficial to later lactation.

HORNY MOOSE

IN the mid-1980s, the *Rutland Herald* followed the affair between a cow and a moose. Jessica was a Shaftsbury cow and was visited by a bull moose who decided to stay with Jessica for some time. It became a very popular site, and articles were written about the two animals who seemed to become partners. Finally, after several weeks the moose left and the game warden in the area was asked why the moose left. He said the moose lost his antlers and he was no longer a "horny" moose.

DAMNED IF I DO AND DAMNED IF I DON'T

I held an agricultural forum in Berlin, Vermont. I invited all my equals from New England as well as a speaker from Welch's Grape Juice, a very successful cooperative. All the New England Cooperatives as well as Vermont legislators were participants. I billed it as a think tank session and asked Governor Kunin to open the session. Some very productive ideas flowed from the session: the dairy compact, additional current use assistance, a dairy subsidy, and other measures. The press called to ask about the session. They said some of the participants said it was only a political show and nothing was going to happen. I said I understood there was politics involved, but the intent was to move forward on many of the recommendations. I asked the press person to use my statement in the article. I said, "I was damned if I did and damned if I didn't, and I don't mind being damned." The next day, the article concerning the session contained my quote as a headline! "Allbee doesn't mind being damned!" The Governor told me she wished she could use the quote!

SHE IS TOO OLD TO HIRE

ONE of the divisional directors in the Agricultural Department in was interviewing candidates for a clerical position. He told me he was interviewing an older woman in the department, but he was not going to consider her because she was too old. I informed him we could not hire based on age and he was not to discuss any age issue with the candidate during the interview. After the interview, he informed me he liked her, but informed her she was too old for the job. I told him due to his stupidity he had just hired her for the position!

HOW MANY TURKEYS DOES VERMONT SEND TO FLORIDA?

WHEN a reporter calls a department, the first thing an employee will do is refer it to another person. Hopefully, a person who can handle the question. In the 1970s, the Agricultural Department referred a *Miami Herald* reporter to my office. The gentleman said he was calling because he had just eaten Vermont turkey at a Miami restaurant. He said Florida had a truth in menu law which required the item he was eating to be a Vermont turkey. At that time, we did not have any slaughterhouses shipping Vermont turkeys, nor did we have a large turkey population. However, I assured him Vermont had a large turkey industry . He was surprised and said he was not aware of that fact. Yes, I said, "They go down in the fall without feathers and come back in the spring without feathers." He laughed as he comprehended my joke. I never knew if he printed his article with my comment.

SAND BAGGING AN ELEVATOR

IRV was commissioner of buildings and grounds for the state of Vermont. He was a real Vermonter who worked his way up to manage the various buildings owned by the state. He was always accommodating and thought of the most pragmatic way to fix things. Like the many legislators and governors, he worked with, he tried to minimize costs and maximize revenue from various sources. Someone reported the elevator in one of the buildings was not stopping at the right spot on a floor. Irv's solution to the problem was to put some sandbags on the roof of the elevator to weigh it down so it stopped at the proper point.

GREEN TURKEY FOR THE GOVERNOR

GREEN turkey's caused Paul to lose his position as Vermont's commissioner of agriculture. In retrospect, while it was a situation which could have been avoided, it could also have happened to me. To help with the promotion of Vermont turkeys during Thanksgiving, the Vermont Agricultural Department produced green labels to be attached to the turkeys after slaughter and before packaging. Unfortunately, no one thought to check if the labels were food protected and would not leak green dye on the turkeys. The green dye on the turkeys became an event. When Governor Kunin held her going away party and we all gave her gifts, I found one of the green turkeys in a department freezer and gave it to her.

SWINGING ON THE TAIL OF A TOOTHLESS TIGER

THE general assembly passes laws, the agencies enact regulations under the laws, and then it is up to the agencies and departments to enforce the laws. I found that sometimes the enforcement is difficult and is usually related to the ability of the inspectors and department officials to carry out their duties. There is no black and white in government; there is much gray. Bureaucracies move slowly, and most people do not like change. I always remind people of what President Truman told an aide as he was leaving the Oval Office. He turned to an aide and said, Isn't Ike going to have fun? He is going to push a button, and nothing is going to happen!"

FILLING POCKETS WITH FOOD

MY two years working for the Vermont legislature provided me with an acute education on the inner workings of government. When I became commissioner (secretary) of agriculture for the state, I was sensitive to the legislative branch. Annually, I would hold a luncheon in the department for the Agricultural Committee members of the General Assembly. It was an opportunity to brief them on the department and the issues we would be discussing with them during the session. A senator who was a good friend would always attend and enjoyed the many varieties of food we provided. One day, as he was leaving, he filled his pockets with food. I laughed to myself as I saw him leave the department.

SUPPLIER OF ARMS IN ST. ALBANS

I am not sure how I obtained the invitation, perhaps through my friend who managed the St. Albans Cooperative. In the late 1970s, I was invited to visit an arms company operating out of a warehouse in St. Albans City. The company imported and exported arms from around the world. They had every conceivable weapon and ammunition going back decades. I was astounded a company existed in Vermont which dealt with arms on such a large scale. Later, I served on the Vermont Economic Development Board as Vermont's commissioner of agriculture. Century Arms submitted an application to the board for funding to expand the business in St. Albans. The board held a lively debate concerning the nature of the business and the implications for the state in lending to an arms supplier. The majority felt the loan was justified. I raised the moral question of a state involving itself in the arms business and voted against the loan. I was the single dissenter on the board. A few years later, a Canadian reporter who had been following the company called me and noted I had been the lone dissenter. He wanted further clarification of my vote which I was happy to give.

PIGEONS DROPPING DEAD ON LAWNS

AS commissioner (secretary) of agriculture, I was responsible for approving pesticide and herbicide permits in Vermont. Thus, when any substance was utilized to kill, it required my approval unless it was a waterway controlled by another agency. One day, the division director came to my office and presented a permit authorizing the poisoning of pigeons at the university farm in South Burlington. Hundreds of pigeons roosted in the barns and caused difficulty for the managers. Thus, the university applied for a permit to poison the pigeons. I asked the director if the level of poison was sufficient to ensure pigeons would not suddenly flop out of the sky onto neighbor's lawns. The farm is situated close to suburban South Burlington. He assured me the level of poison had been calculated to ensure no pigeons would end up on lawns. A new governor had been elected, and my replacement had been selected. I knew I had an out. I told the director the permit could await the signature of my replacement since I was not confident pigeons would not end up on lawns. About two months after my replacement took office, I turned on the television to Channel 3 News in Burlington. The reporter was announcing residents of South Burlington had awakened to pigeons falling on their lawns and dying. I was happy my successor had to manage the aftermath.

MY COWS LEAVE SOMETHING BEHIND

FRANCIS was a successful farmer of Irish heritage who owned several dairy farms in Franklin County, Vermont. He utilized his innate grassroots abilities to hone through the basis of any legislative proposal. Governors often underestimated his legislative abilities. In the mid-1980s, Governor Kunin proposed legislation to create the Housing and Conservation Board and adjustments to regional planning. The legislation easily passed the house, and a Senate vote was looming. The governor's staff made their count and were one vote short... Senator Howrigan's. She invited Francis into her state house office to lobby for his vote. She also invited me, knowing Francis and I had a respectful relationship. I was not one to force his hand, as it would be a waste of my energy. I looked forward to the encounter and knew any negotiations with the senator would not be easy. Francis normally wore a suit with a few food stains. He walked in and said, "Nice outfit, Governor." She returned the compliment and said, "Nice suit, Senator." She told Francis the legislation was the cornerstone of her legislation, and she was asking for his vote. In typical fashion, he said he wasn't sure he could vote for the measure. She asked him why. He said farmers needed some property tax relief, and if she would provide additional monies for tax relief, he could vote for the legislation. She said all the money had been appropriated, and nothing was left for tax relief. He said he was disappointed. "Governor, you know I am a farmer whose cows sometimes get into the corn. They always leave something behind!" All he was asking her to do was leave something behind. She said that she would consider his request and the meeting was over. Francis received the money for tax relief and voted for the legislation.

After a successful Senate vote, the governor's staff and I celebrated with drinks at the Thrush Tavern. Discussion centered on the members of the Conference Committee who would negotiate the differences in the house and Senate versions of the legislation. The governor's staff assured me Senator Howrigan would not be an appointed member of the Conference Committee. I asked how they came by the information and was told the governor received names from the speaker and the Senate leadership. I knew nothing about conference committee membership negotiations, but I did know Francis. I suggested Francis would be on the committee and would bet anyone a fine bottle of whiskey. They took my bet with the confidence of a win.

The next day's Free Press headlined "Howrigan Appointed to Conference Committee." I went to visit Francis and asked how he arranged the appointment. He told me it was secured about four weeks before the Senate vote. Francis outfoxed the governor and did not leave anything behind. I received my bottle of whiskey from the governor's staff.

GRADE B, MAPLE PRODUCERS, IMPORTS FROM CANADA

VERMONT is the largest producer of Maple syrup in the United States, and the Agricultural Agency is the regulator of the product. The leadership of the Maple industry asked me to change the grading system for grade B. Several leaders joined me in my office to argue for the change, and a large canner Newport, Vt led the group. He stood out as a leader of the group, but was later convicted of altering the product, and his company failed. Later, some of the same leaders came in and were complaining about the amount of Canadian syrup imported into the states from Canada. As I listened to them, I asked the chief inspector to bring down the U.S. Custom's list of Vermont importers of Canadian syrup. I found some of their names on the documents and showed them the list. They were embarrassed I had the information and quietly left my office.

COW PLOP CONTEST

MY family helped start the New Brooke Fire Department in Newfane and Brookline during the 1940s when they realized neither town could successfully operate their own fire department. The family sawmill supplied the lumber for the firehouse, and the construction equipment was always available to provide necessary services. One of the many fundraising activities for the fire department was August Field Days held in a field south of the Newfane Village. The normal fair activities were available as well as horse-drawing contests, horse shows, and fireworks. It was one of the main activities for the valley during August, and it was an exciting place to be on an August night in the West River Valley. The field days were my heritage. Joe Nichols called me and asked me to judge a cow plop contest. I could not refuse the request. Where else would a Secretary of Agriculture for a state judge a cow plop contest. "What is a cow plop contest?" They cordon off a corral and place grids inside. People buy tickets for each lined grid, much like a checkerboard. If the cow defecates or plops in your grid, you win. It works much like a game in Las Vegas except it depends on cow feces. I appeared at the contest with my father and learned my cousin Howard was bringing a cow from his farm. Howard appeared with a horse van and a cow. The cow was led into the ring and she laid down. The contest lasted two hours, and the cow never moved from its spot the entire time. The cow was unable to produce the required plop. They declared the contest over and told everyone they would get their money back. My father said it was certainly a Vermont cow. I asked him why. He said the cow was shy, frugal, and conservative. Truly, a Vermont cow.

PREGNANT COW

I was asked to judge the contest again the next year. My cousin again brought the cow. This time, the cow was obviously very pregnant or full of "shit." In about an hour, the cow decided she was going to give birth. She laid down and started birthing – with all the outsiders who had never seen a cow deliver looking on. It was obviously a breech birth, and help was needed. My cousin Howard grabbed a rope, and I helped him pull the calf from the cow in front of the onlookers. Fortunately, there was no press and no reporters who could write about the Secretary of Agriculture pulling a calf from a cow.

AGRICULTURAL DEVELOPMENT AND EXTENSION, THE SILOS

GOVERNOR Salmon appointed a food commission in 1974 to study agriculture in Vermont. The commission identified the changing agriculture and made many recommendations. I was staffing the legislative agricultural committees who were reviewing the many recommendations. Marketing was identified as one of the weaknesses in Vermont agricultural delivery services. I helped the legislature develop legislation creating an Agricultural Development Division in the Department of Agriculture and provide for the development of a Vermont seal of quality. The legislation easily passed the legislature, and those involved eagerly awaited the department's fulfillment of the legislative requirements.

Due to the unexpected death of the deputy commissioner, I was appointed deputy commissioner and charged with implementing the legislation. The department was a regulatory agency and creating a marketing arm within the Agency was a challenge. Gil Parker, an able long-term employee who knew everything and everybody in Vermont agriculture, was selected as the division director. I recognized the creation of the division was not looked at favorably by the UVM extension service and its director. Gil and his assistant took the reins and beginning assisting in the development of farmers' markets, new marketing channels, and education functions for new entrants. It was a beginning that would lead to further marketing efforts including development of Vermont organic standards, new cooperatives, cheese facilities, diversified Vermont products, etc. In the end, the extension service and the department were able to tear down the silos and work together as they had historically.

COMMODORE OF LAKE CHAMPLAIN

SEVERAL of us knew Governor Kunin before she became governor. When she was preparing to depart, she decided to have a going away party at Seyon Ranch in Groton, Vermont. Seyon is a state park, and many governors used the facility for staff retreats. The lodge is located on the edge of Seyon Pond, a brook trout fly-fishing only pond. After we had partied into the evening, the governor stated she would love to learn how to fly fish. I told her I had brought my fly rod, and if she were up by 8:00 a.m., I would take her fly fishing on the pond. At 8:00 a.m. the next morning, we boarded the rowboat, and I set her up with my fishing equipment while I rowed. It was her first time, and she was having some difficulty with the technique. She suggested she row while I fished. The governor started rowing around the pond while I fished. People in other boats were asking if it is the governor rowing the boat. I said it was the governor. I know they are wondering how you get the governor of the state to row a boat while you fly fish? She said she was prepared to assist me after we leave office. I thanked her and told her there was something she could do for me. Don Edwards was the adjutant general who was appointed by the legislature. I told her I served in the navy in Vietnam and would like to become the commodore of Lake Champlain. Not missing a beat, she said her husband Arthur wanted to become commodore. Of course, there was no such position.

AMOUNT OF FOOD IMPORTED

SOMETIME in the middle 1980s, I read in the paper Vermont imported 85% of its food. I was anxious to find out where the statistic came from and traced it to two people associated with Vermont agriculture. I asked them for references for the information, and they said there was none. They were having lunch one afternoon, and they asked each other how much food was imported. Each agreed 85% was probably the correct figure. That is how information is sometimes generated! Statistics lie and liars use statistics.

HE'S AWFULLY LIBERAL, ISN'T HE?

THE governor appoints the commissioner of agriculture in Vermont and many of the northeast states. In many of the southern states the commissioners run for office and serve many years; they have their own power base. Such was the case in the state of Mississippi where the commissioner had served for decades. The state commissioners were holding their annual meeting in Washington, D.C., and they asked me to extend an invitation to my old boss, Senator Leahy. The senator agreed, and I was given the courtesy of introducing him. I was sitting next to the commissioner from Mississippi, and he leaned over to me and said, "Your senator is awfully liberal, isn't he?" I felt like telling him Vermont opposed slavery in the 1800s, and it just runs through our veins!

VERMONT OCCUPATIONAL AND SAFETY

BOB Brannon served as senator from Franklin County, and upon the retirement of Leo O'Brien as commissioner of agriculture, Bob became commissioner. After the deputy commissioner of agriculture was tragically killed in a motor vehicle accident, Bob asked me to become his deputy. About a week later, Bob came to me and said, "You might want to reconsider." I asked him why. He said, "I've just been diagnosed with liver cancer, and I have from six to eight months to live." I told him I was sorry and would still accept the position.

I was travelling to Franklin County quite frequently briefing Bob on the actions in the agricultural agency. OSHA, Occupational Safety was proposing safety regulations for farms. A gentleman in VOSHA, the Vermont safety unit, offered to go visit farms with myself and see how they might affect farms. I called the extension agent in Franklin County, and arranged for three or four farms to visit, one of the farms being the commissioner's.

We visited the three or four farms looking for such things as no PTO guards, lack of guards, other equipment, etc. We came to the commissioner's farm, and there were no guards on any PTO equipment. He also had a welder with no plug, just bare wires he placed in the socket!

When I got home, I called the agent and said, "You SOB, why the hell did you set me up with the commissioner knowing full well the farm was operated in that manner?" We were friends so we could get away with those discussions. I never told the commissioner how bad his farm was since the regulations weren't going into effect. I did tell him he might want to change his welder and put a real plug on it.

FIDDLIN' FARMER

THE farm cooperative meetings in the 1970s always included entertainment. One of the strangest entertainers was the Fiddling' Farmer who would play the fiddle with his feet. He was quite an accomplished foot fiddler.

VIETNAM OF VERMONT STATE GOVERNMENT

WHEN a governor makes a new appointment, the person appears with him or her at a press conference. Such was the case when Governor Kunin appointed me to replace Paul Stone as commissioner of agriculture. The press corps was lined up around the table in the pavilion conference room, and the governor finished introducing me and opened it up to questions. One of the first questions came from Tim who was the WCAX reporter. He asked how I was going to deal with a department known as the Vietnam of Vermont State Government. I said it would not be a problem since I was a veteran of Vietnam.

WHAT DO THEY CALL YOU?

THE press called shortly after my appointment and asked what the staff in the department called me. I said at regular functions they call me commissioner. In the office they call me Ron and on other occasions they probably call me many things!

NEED TO UNDERSTAND MILK PRICING.

DURING the 1987 legislative session, a debate ensued concerning prices paid to dairy farmers. The legislature was considering many measures to improve the welfare of Vermont dairy farmers and the overall industry. Governor Kunin was enmeshed in the controversy and at one point asked me to educate her on dairy pricing. I said it was very complicated and the man who developed the system once told me it was developed "so no one could understand the system." She insisted on the education. I arranged for Dr. Fred Webster at the University of Vermont and Ryle Dow, the manager of St. Albans Cooperative to meet at the governor's office at 5:30 p.m. Both were experts of the arcane system and started discussing the system with the governor. After about twenty-five minutes ,she said she had a terrible headache and had to excuse herself. I wanted to say, "I told you so."

WHY AREN'T YOU GOING ON
THE GOVERNOR'S TRIP?

SHORTLY after Dick Snelling took office as a first-term governor, he announced a sister state relation with a state in Switzerland. The purpose of the visit was to establish trade ties with the other state. In his announcement, he stated he would be taking selected state officials on the trip. The announcement was in the *Burlington Free Press*. I decided to have a little fun after the announcement. My friend was serving as Vermont's labor commissioner, and my twin brother was working for the Environmental Agency and had a little office in the Tavern Hotel. Across the hall from Roger was Peg Garland, an aide to Governor Snelling. Peg was a tall and accomplished woman who served in the woman air corps during World war II ferrying planes to Europe. Bill Gilbert was serving as the governor's principal assistant. I called my friend the Labor Commissioner and said, why aren't you on the governor's list? I am on the list." There was no list, and he knew immediately I was pulling his leg. So, he called Peg and said, "Peg, Ron Allbee and I are on the governor's list, why aren't you on the list?" Peg immediately called Bill Gilbert and demanded to know why she was not on the list. Of course, Bill figured out we were pulling her leg!

SHE DIDN'T BELIEVE HE WAS A SENATOR
AND I WAS THE COMMISSIONER!

THE department participated every holiday season in Christmas in Cambridge. Several Vermont vendors would set up around the Cambridge Inn with their wares, and the inn would advertise the festivities. One year, I carried some *Vermont Life* magazines to hand out to attendees. I was standing at a Vermont booth, and I noticed Vince , a Vermont state senator at another booth selling Christmas wreaths with a family from the Newport, Vermont area. Vince was trying to sell a wreath to a very proper Cambridge lady. I went over with a *Vermont Life* magazine and heard him telling her he was a Vermont state senator. When I arrived, he pointed to me and said, "This is our commissioner of agriculture." She said, "I have heard enough," and stormed off!

SAFEST PLACE IN THE WORLD

IN the mid-1970s, Venezuelans were buying up Vermont farm and forest properties. I contacted one of the real estate brokers fronting for the purchases and inquired about the background of the purchases. I asked why Vermont, the land does not necessary lend itself to the kind of farming they were familiar with in their own country? The answer I received surprised me. He told me they were looking for a safe place in the world, and they concluded that Vermont was one of the safest places. Although I loved Vermont, I never considered it one of the safest places in the world.

Vermont Energy Director - 1978 to 1980

ENERGY OFFICE

THE Vermont State Energy Office was created after the first energy crisis in the early 1970s. It was funded by a grant provided by the U.S. Energy Department, and its director was appointed by and accountable to the governor of Vermont. I was appointed director by Governor Snelling in 1978, just prior to the second energy crisis.

CARTOON AND BILLY CARTER

I collected cartoons I would cut out and place on the bulletin board in my office. My secretary was prudish and removed cartoons she thought distasteful. Carter was president, and his brother Billy always seemed to get in trouble. Billy ran into trouble when he signed as a lobbyist for Libya. He was banned from the White House and forced to give up his lucrative career. Instead, he went into the beer business producing "Billy Beer." One of my favorite cartoons showed the White House lit up on a snowy day with snow on the ground. Tracks led up to the front of the White House where the word "Billy" was written in yellow. The tracks then led away from the White House. Most people who saw the cartoon figured out it was meant to be Billy peeing in the snow in front of the White House. It did not take my secretary long to remove the cartoon!

THREE-MILE ISLAND

THE incident at Three Mile Island's nuclear plant in Pennsylvania caused a reconsideration of nuclear power. Many politicians were reconsidering their support of nuclear power in light of the incident. Governor King served as a Republican governor of Massachusetts. Governor Snelling and I flew in Snelling's plane to Logan Airport to meet with Governor King and his staff concerning energy. Snelling, an excellent pilot, flew his twin-engine craft into Logan, taxied to the waiting area where the Massachusetts state police met us. We were whisked through the streets to the state house for a press conference with Governor King. Governor Snelling, a normal supporter of nuclear power, said he would await an investigation into the situation before making further conclusions about nuclear power. King, on the other hand, was less concerned and stated he did not care about the details of the three-mile incident; he still strongly supported nuclear energy. We were quickly escorted to the police cars and taken to the airport and flew back to Vermont. I was appalled, but not surprised by Governor King's actions.

POWER OF THE GOVERNORS IN MASSACHUSETTS

MONTHLY, the other New England directors and our counterparts in Canada, would meet in various states and provinces. We arranged to meet in Boston. It was the responsibility of the staff in the host community to make the hosting arrangements. My friend Fred, who worked for the Massachusetts energy office, made arrangements for us to eat in the north end at a well-known Italian restaurant. We arrived at the restaurant and Fred told the maître d' he had reservations. The maître d' checked his book and said there were no reservations for the party. Fred insisted he made the reservations, and again was refused. The restaurant was full, and we were not going to be provided either a table or food. Fred was embarrassed at the inconvenience. He asked to see the owner and told the maître d' he was with the governor's office and the guests were guests of the governor. He said it would be unfortunate if he told the governor of his experiences at the restaurant. Fred took the opportunity to speak kindly to the owner. Suddenly, not only did a table open, but we were provided some of the best Italian food and wine at on the House.

SCARE NEW ENGLAND

MONTHLY, I flew out of the Montpelier airport to meet with my fellow energy directors at the New England Regional Commission in Boston. A small airline called Air New England served the Vermont to Boston corridor. I called the small airline "Scare New England." I was always reluctant to travel on a foggy day or in inclement weather. The airline pilots followed the interstates to Boston, and if the weather were inclement, they lost their signposts.

DIDN'T WE HAVE A GOOD TIME LAST NIGHT?

ROGER was working for Congressman Jeffords in Washington for the Agricultural Committee, and I was traveling to Washington at least once per month on energy and other related matters. One morning, I was making my way to a meeting and was traveling on the subway. I exited the subway and was making my way up the side when this young woman came running up, hugged me, and said, "Roger, didn't we have a great time last evening?" I assured her we did and should repeat the experience that evening! I later learned Congressman Jeffords had a staff party the evening before, and she had confused me with my twin.

CAN'T DO IT

I made the mistake of publicly suggesting the state needed an energy plan. It was just before Memorial Day, and my annual fishing trip with friends to Island Pond was planned. The Governor called me into his office and said he wanted a draft energy plan on his desk the following Monday. He was not pleased to read my suggestion in the news. I said I could not meet his directive and expected a further dressing down. He asked me why, and I told him. He said he wished he could go fishing that weekend and I suggested he join us. He said he had speeches to give and I could prepare a plan when I returned. I did return and never prepared a plan, as I knew there was a justification for not having a plan.

NAME LEFT OUT OF PHONE BOOK

A new phone book was published for the Barre/Montpelier area and my name and phone number were missing. My wife called the phone company and was told we did not pay our phone bill. It was not the appropriate response for we were always timely in payments, and the company had obviously messed up. They said nothing could be done to correct the error. I knew it was a lie and asked my friend who served as chairperson of the Public Service Commission for the remedy. He told me the utility was required to adjust our bill during the year. I called the company with the information, and they apologized and told me I was correct. They said the correction would be made the following year. The phone book came out the second year with no name or number. Again, I called, and was told it would be corrected the third year. It was corrected the third year.

THEY PUT THEIR PANTS ON SAME WAY I DO

TODAY, it is hard to believe that there was an energy crisis in the 1970s when OPEC controlled the price and supply of oil. I accompanied Governor Snelling to the White House on two occasions when the governors met to discuss energy issues. The first meeting was with President Carter, Vice President Mondale, and the northeast governors in the cabinet room of the White House. Each governor was allowed to bring one aide. Snelling's father was a scientist in energy and the governor was well-versed in the issues. As I stood there watching and listening, I came to realize neither the president nor the vice president had any more idea how to solve the crisis than the governor nor I. Carter was not wearing his famous sweater at the meeting.

The next meeting was a luncheon meeting with all the governors in one of the main White House dining rooms. Again, Carter spoke before the group as did his Secretary of Energy, Secretary Schlesinger. Jerry Brown was the young governor of California and threatening to run against the president. Jerry was pontificating at the meeting and quite literally making himself a policy irritant.

SMOKING POT IN CANADA

DURING the period 1978 to 1980, the northeastern Canadian premiers and the New England governors met at least quarterly. Sometimes, the meetings were held in the states, and at other times, they were held in Canada. It was an interesting time, particularly when we met in Montreal and Rene Leveque was premier. He and Governor Snelling became good friends and it was interesting to watch them interact. After one of the meetings in Quebec, the staffs met to follow up on the details of the meeting. One of the Canadian staffers pulled out a marijuana cigarette and started passing it around. It was my first experience with marijuana, and while it was novel, I did not have any sensation. Perhaps, like former President Clinton, I did not inhale!

FIRE AT THE ENERGY OFFICE

THE Vermont state energy office was located on upper State Street on the second floor of a building which housed an old bowling alley. A liquor store and children's store were downstairs and upstairs housed the energy office, the veteran's affairs office, part of the attorney general's office, and the office for the sheriff's association. The energy office utilized most of the upstairs. It was the last day of work before the New Year's holiday, and we hosted a party for the many residents of the building. After the party, we left all the booze in one of the many offices. Slightly before the liquor store closed, the fire chief came in to purchase liquor. He told the clerk he smelled something and was told it was a normal smell. Slightly later, one of my friends purchased some liquor and was told the same thing. The store closed, and a few hours later, I received a call informing me my office was on fire. When the fire alarm started, the fire department came out of the building on Main Street and turned left instead of right. By the time they corrected their error, the building was engulfed in flames. We watched as they tried to save as much of the building as possible. The following day, I looked for a temporary location for the energy office. Shortly thereafter, the State Buildings Director called me as asked if I would like to help pay for a large crane to reclaim some of the items in the building. I told him I considered everything in the energy office lost and would not try to recover anything. He said veteran's affairs wanted their charred documents. They would place the crane on the street and try to recover documents. On the appointed day, they placed the crane next to the burned-out building. I watched as the first desk/filing cabinet was pulled from the building and placed on the street. The desk and cabinet were completely charred as they laid them in the middle of East State Street. They pried open the lower door on the desk and out came charred "girlie magazines." What an expensive way to find charred magazines. We never identified the owner of the desk.

SKI AREA AND ENERGY CONSERVATION

AFTER I resigned as energy director, a couple of the employees and I established Energy Solutions, an energy consulting company. I knew the owner of Bolton Valley Ski Area and secured a contract to review their energy usage and provide him with recommendations. We were reviewing one of the condos. The manager told us he thought they were energy efficient. The consulting engineer lit a match in the unit, and the wind blowing against the building extinguished the match.

CHAPTER 10

TEACHING

ARE TESTS ANY GOOD?

I was employed part-time teaching micro and macroeconomics at Norwich University in Northfield, Vermont. Most students were in their sophomore year. Economics is a dismal sciences which does not come naturally to most students. I taught them and followed up with quizzes. I went over the answers afterward. The quizzes were for educational purposes in preparation for their hour exams, and therefore did not carry much weight. I followed the lead of a friend's father who taught economics at Harvard University. I gave them quizzes and went over the answers to the quizzes. I gave the same questions on the hour exams. I thought it gave students the opportunity for higher grade and provide them with the means to further understand economics. I was surprised when I corrected the first hour exams. I was astonished when I corrected the second hour exams. The test scores were such it appeared they did not study for the exams or utilize the quizzes in their studies. I inquired as to how they studied for the exams and found the answer, "Very little!"

I CAN'T READ

I would give hourly exams to the mostly sophomore economic students. One student failed the first test, and his writing was hardly legible. It was evident he did not comprehend the questions. I put a note on his test and asked him to visit me in my office. He failed to do so before I gave a second hourly exam. The results on the second exam were the same, and I walked up to him and asked him to meet me in my office after the class. I asked him why he was having a problem. He told me he could not read. The teachers in high school had continued to pass him. At that time, the university did not have entrance requirements for students and were filling their dorms. Those who did not make the grade would leave at the end of their sophomore year. Many universities and colleges were filling their dorms without any concern for the individual student and his or her abilities. Norwich was not alone.

WHERE IS THE FEMALE MOOSE?

IT was a nice spring day and the windows were open. As I was lecturing, one of the students let out a very loud yawn and startled everyone in the room. I slowly walked over to the window and looked out. The room was quiet, and all the students wondered what was about to happen. I looked to my left and to my right and slowly brought my head back into the classroom. I said, "I didn't see it"! One student said, what did you not see Mr. Allbee? I said I did not see the female moose as that was a bull moose call, I heard in the classroom. They all erupted in laughter and I was able to continue lecturing.

CHAPTER 11

CONSULTING AND BUSINESS

DAIRY COOPERATIVE POLITICS

AS much as I enjoy farmers, I could never understand why dairy politics were so rough and tumble. I suspect was due the farmer's independence. They joked and drank together and went to their separate cooperatives and fought. I became enmeshed in the politics when I became deputy commissioner of agriculture. One event comes to mind. In the early 1980s, Congress passed a national dairy promotional program and provided there would be a National Dairy Board with members appointed by the president. The dairy cooperatives in New England were anxious to have one of their members become the first regional appointee to the board. I was consulting with the Green Mountain Dairy Federation which included St. Albans and Cabot. Agri-Mark, the larger New England Cooperative submitted their candidate's name which was on the president's desk. They were quite certain their well-qualified business member would be the appointee. At the last minute, the board of the federation asked me to submit the name of their candidate. I knew I was playing catch-up and a Hail Mary would be necessary. I remembered former Governor Deane Davis served with President Reagan and were friends. I also knew my candidate had worked with Governor Davis on dairy and other matters over the years. I called Governor Davis, explained the situation, and asked if he would intervene on behalf of my candidate. He indicated he would be pleased to do so. In a matter of days, my candidate became the presidential appointee to the National Dairy Board. I was sorry I had to defeat the other candidate, for he was a fine fellow and would have served with distinction.

WILL THE SENATOR STAY FOR THE HEARING?

SENATOR Leahy and other politicians were often calling on my friend, the President of Cabot Cooperative for advice. The senator invited him to Washington to testify at a hearing on dairy legislation. This was his first experience in Washington testifying before a committee. On the way to Washington, he asked me what would happen at the hearing. I told him prior to the start of the hearing the senator would take several pictures with him and other farmers. Once the hearing started, the senators in attendance would praise each other's abilities and commitment to agriculture. I said that Senator Leahy would be there for his presentation, but following that, he might leave to attend to other business. Pat was not sure I was giving him the entire script. Everything I told him followed my script.

DON'T WORRY, I KNOW HIM!

ST. Albans Cooperative was a successfully dairy cooperative located in St. Albans, Vermont. An intelligent man and dairy leader managed the cooperative. They held their monthly meetings at the cooperative headquarters and afterward retired for drinks and dinner at the Cornerstone Restaurant. Most farmers did not drink milk for dinner but choose a drink with more kick. After dinner they retired to a vehicle to return to the headquarters and were pulled over by a city policeman. One of the board members told the others not to worry; he knew the policeman and would take care of the issue. He exited the vehicle to take care of the issue. The policeman decided all were sufficiently inebriated and locked them up for the evening. The next day, the local newspaper ran a story about the board being locked up overnight.

WHAT YOU SAW AND HEARD AT FARM MEETINGS

ONE could never predict what he would hear or see at farm meetings. The meetings were an opportunity for members to learn about dairy prices, market information, animal health, and production issues. I learned a farmer would never admit he or she was making money. For most, it was always a bad year! Sometimes, there were spirited debates over dairy policies. Often, there was music or entertainment provided. I remember the farmer who played the violin with his feet. Or the farmer who always wore kilts to meetings. Lunches or dinners were provided, and attending farmers asked few questions. After one dairy promotional meeting (lunch) where several hundreds of thousands were approved, I asked the director how he pulled off such an accomplishment. I was told it was important to provide a lunch or dinner, and fewer questions would be asked. After one cooperative meeting, I listened to a manager skirt over some important issues without any questions. I could see some farmers were unsettled by what they were being told. When I returned to my office, a farmer called and wanted to know why I did not ask the appropriate questions. I told him he, not I, was a member of the cooperative and he should ask the questions.

NEWBURY, VERMONT'S MURDER

IN the 1960s, a Newbury, Vermont farmer was allegedly beating his wife and hired man. One day, his body was found floating in the Connecticut River. There was a vigilante action, and the FBI and state police tried to solve the case with no success. No one in the town ever talked. One of the farmers allegedly involved moved to St. Albans, Vermont and purchased a farm. He became actively involved in the St. Albans Cooperative. My friend was the manager of the cooperative and told me he would always try to get the farmer drunk after cooperative meetings and ply him about the event. He could never get him to talk, and he, like most of those involved in Newbury, took the story to their grave.

SIGNAGE ON BUSINESS

IN 1990, I was part of starting Cheesetraders, a business selling cheeses, wines, gourmet, and discount foods on Williston Road in South Burlington. The business was located in a large two-story building with a front façade facing the road. We had a large sign made with large black letters and a yellow background and placed it on the façade. Not long after, we received a visit from the South Burlington zoning/sign inspector informing us the sign was not legal and violated their ordinance due to its size. I asked him if we painted the entire façade the color of the sign background, so the letters were only visible, would we still be in violation. He told me we would then be in conformance since the letters alone were not large enough to violate the ordinance. For me, it was an exhibition of the difficulty and the absurdity of some ordinances and regulations.

I AM GOING TO CLOSE YOU DOWN!

IN the mid-1980s, my then wife and I decided to switch careers and purchase a food business in Brattleboro, Vermont. Prior to purchasing the business from the seller, it was inspected by the health department to ensure there were no violations. Within two weeks of our purchase. the inspector showed up again to conduct another inspection. This time, the inspector informed myself and my wife there was a violation in the sink drainage, and she was going to close us down until it was fixed. I asked how she could approve it two weeks ago and tell us she was going to close us down now. She said that the regulations had changed. I asked if other facilities were in violation, and she said they probably were. I asked her to wait while I made a call. She asked me whom I was going to call. I told her I was going to call the local press and have them follow us to other facilities in town in violation and also close them down, as by her own admission they were also in violation. At that point, she asked me to stop. She said she would not close the facility, but I should correct the violation. I thanked her, and she never addressed the issue again nor did I fix the violation. However, I felt sorry for the poor businessperson who had no government experience!

I CAN KILL YOU

CHEESETRADERS was a large food store in South Burlington that I and two other partners started in 1990 after I left as commissioner of agriculture and after my separation from my first wife. The store was a success, and we hired over twenty full- and part-time employees. One of the part-time employees was a former Korean kickboxer who lived with his sister in Burlington. The man started developing paranoia about the other employees, believing they did not like him and were out to get him. I called him into my office to talk about his concerns, and he started telling me about his kickboxing in Korea. I had a container on my desk with pencils, and the kickboxer picked up a pencil and said, "See this pencil, I could kill you with it." He was quite serious, and I told him he could leave for the day. I then called his sister and talked to her about the incident and her brother's reactions to other employees. The boxer did not return to work but was placed in the mental ward at the hospital where his medications were corrected.

KNOWING WHERE YOUR FOOD COMES FROM

TODAY, the public goes to a grocery store to purchase food without any knowledge of its origins. I am alarmed by the public's lack of knowledge, and when I have an opportunity, I enjoy testing their knowledge. My twin brother and I were selling cheese in the Vermont Building at the Eastern States Exposition. Green Mountain Coffee also exhibited in the building. One day, a woman was walking by with a cup of Green Mountain Coffee. I asked her if she enjoyed the coffee. She said she enjoyed the coffee and it was some of the best she had consumed. I told her she was lucky, because Vermont only has one crop in the Green Mountain state every four years. She asked me why, and I told her that the climate was the problem. She asked me where it was grown in Vermont, and I told her in Bennington County because it gets some warmth from New York state. She seemed to accept my logic and moved on.

URINE SAMPLE

DEBBIE managed the downstairs of Cheesetraders. Downstairs featured broken case lots and closely dated grocery items. Weekly, we would receive at least a trailer of banana boxes loaded with grocery items requiring sorting and cleaning before being placed on the shelves. It was hard and dirty work. Debbie asked if I would interview her brother for a job as he was being released from state prison. I ended up hiring Mike to work downstairs sorting and handling the hundreds of banana boxes. Shortly thereafter, she approached me about hiring another brother who was facing jail time for failure to pay child support. Again, I hired her brother Bill to work downstairs. Bill always wore sunglasses to hide the redness in his eyes from smoking pot. They both proved to be wonderful workers, diligently performing the difficult tasks of sorting and moving groceries. Bill loved driving the forklift and moving the boxes off the trailer trucks. One day he came to me and said the forklift had damaged the bumper of a car parked in the back of the store. I went down and looked at the car to find a minor dent. Bill was asked to find the customer so we could provide the insurance information. I decided to have some fun with Bill and found a good customer who I knew would enjoy a little levity. I gave the customer an empty jar and asked him to tell Bill he was the insurance adjuster and Bill should provide a urine sample and bring it to Ron. A short time later, Bill appeared with the full yellow bottle and said, "It is not going to pass, Ron."

FOR BETTER OR WORSE

ESSEX, New York is a small community across the lake from Charlotte, Vermont. In the summer, it is a popular destination for those wanting to enjoy the lake and the quiet community life. One summer, a British friend who operated a bed and breakfast announced she was marrying an old British friend. Her intended was evidently a very successful gentleman in his professional life. The wedding was held in the local Episcopal Church, and many of her Essex friends were invited. We all sat in the church watching the wedding They came to the part where the bride is asked if she "takes this man for rich or poorer, till death do us part." The bride could only say rich; the word "poorer" she was unable to say. We all laughed at her inability to say "poorer."

THEY LAUGHED WHEN I VISITED MY FRIEND

ONE of my dear friends was rushed to the hospital suffering dizziness when she was in her nineties. A friend went to visit and asked for her at the front desk. When he mentioned her name, the front desk personnel started giggling amongst themselves. He was surprised, for she was a very proper woman and would never cause anyone to laugh at her expense. He asked her why they laughed when he mentioned her name. "Well," she said, "I was confused when they checked me in and asked me several questions. They asked if I had ever had surgery. I told them I had broken a leg when I was younger and skied." They said that was not surgery. Had I had surgery? I told them I had a vasectomy when I was in my fifties. Of course, she meant mastectomy!

ENGLISH WINE… CHEESETRADER'S GINGER

WHEN I owned and operated Cheesetraders in South Burlington, we were often buying closeout and overstocked wines from distributors. Once we purchased fifty to sixty cases of a high-end English ginger wine which did not satisfy the palates of Vermonters. We stacked the wine high in the store, and I placed a sign on the wine that said, "Try it before you buy a case. You can use it to cook, you can drink it, or you can use it for a bath rub." The cases lasted a week!

MISS CHEESECAKE

MY brother and I sold cheese and cheesecakes at the Vermont Building at Eastern States Exposition in Springfield, Massachusetts. It was 17 days of hell, and during that time we sold over 20,000 pounds of cheese. It was an intense time, and we decided to have a little fun. The governor was coming to visit so we dressed my brother up as "Miss Cheesecake." He looked quite attractive in his "Miss Cheesecake" outfit. When the governor arrived, Roger went with the governor and his entourage to tour the building. He even planted a big kiss on one of the Vermont agriculture department employees who was part of the tour. Later, we discussed the occurrence with the Commissioner of Agriculture. We lamented Leon did not make the visit as he also would have had a kiss from Miss Cheesecake. Leon did not enjoy the joke and was a little offended. No sense of humor!

HOW CAN ANYONE AS FAT AS YOU TASTE ANYTHING

OUR Vermont cheese booth at Eastern States focused mainly on Cabot cheese. However, we did sell other cheeses and sometimes had people from those companies handing out samples. One day, a representative from a Vermont goat cheese company was handing out samples. A very fat man grabbed a sample and immediately spit it out. The representative replied, "How can someone as fat and rotund as you have a palate that can discern good from bad." Fortunately, the crowd was pushed along so the rotund person had no chance to respond or grab a different variety of cheese.

GERI AND NURSING HOME AND TAXES

MY 100-year old friend was going through rehabilitation at the Elizabethtown Nursing Home in Elizabethtown, New York. At that time the home, the hospital, and the county jail were attached. They were all served from the same kitchen. One day when I visited my friend, she was complaining about the services. She had recently been moved from the hospital to the nursing home. I told her she should not complain too loudly, for the next move could be to the county jail. She laughed and said maybe the services would be better!

COUNTRY GENTLEMAN

WHEN we ran a bed and breakfast in Essex, New York, one of our friends was a pretend weekend farmer. He was a lawyer in NYC, and on weekends he would wear his farmer overalls. He graduated from Texas A&M and pretended to be a country person on weekends, even playing the part by wearing farmer coveralls. Susan and I raised chickens to provide fresh eggs to the guests. During the day, the chickens ran free to gather the bugs in our large garden. One day, our friend drove into our yard, jumped out of the car with his overalls on, and started to the doorway. The chickens saw him and started running toward him, as they were very friendly chickens. He saw the chickens and immediately ran to his car, locked the door, and drove away. We learned that despite his coveralls and appearance of being a farmer, he was afraid of chickens.

CHAPTER 12

FEDERAL GOVERNMENT

OTHER than the service, my federal government employment consisted of working for Senator Patrick Leahy as an agricultural advisor and managing the Vermont/Virgin Islands offices of the Farm Service Agency.

U.S. Senate

◇◇◇◇◇◇◇◇◇◇◇◇◇

WHAT IS THE U.S. SENATE?

IN 1984, U.S. Senator Patrick Leahy asked me to serve as his agricultural advisor in Washington. My wife and I had moved our family from Barre, Vermont to Brattleboro, Vermont where we had purchased a small gourmet food store. My wife quit her position teaching Spanish and French at Norwich University in Northfield, Vermont, and I had discontinued my lobbying position for a group of dairy cooperatives in Vermont (Cabot, St. Albans, Northern Farms). We had resettled, and I could not agree to a position which would again require a move of my family and the sale of a business we had just purchased. The senator was up for re-election in 1986, and after a near defeat in 1980, he was in no mood to take chances. All eyes would be on him as he, a member of the Senate Agricultural Committee, was critical to Vermont's dairy industry as the farm bill was debated. His chief of staff was calling and visiting encouraging me to help the senator as the farm bill proceeded. We agreed I would work an average of three days per week. Some of my time would be spent in Montpelier, Vermont, and when the farm bill was debated, I would travel to Washington, D.C. and stay for the week. As time went on, my travels to Washington became more frequent. I would leave from the train station in Brattleboro, Vermont Sunday evening and arrive in Washington, D.C. the next morning at

Union Station. It was a short walk from the station to the Russell Senate Office Building.

It was one of those periods when dairy prices were low and dairy farmers were again struggling against the tide of milk flowing from the West. The days in Washington were long… meeting with staff to discuss dairy issues and negotiating with the staff of the other Senate offices who might be interested in sugar, wheat, cotton, or corn. There were Senate hearings where agricultural leaders from across the country were invited to testify. Many of the farm leaders and farmers in Vermont and New England were calling to keep updated about the latest developments in the legislation. At the end of the long day, I would return the many calls. One day, I returned a call to a dairy farmer in St. Albans, Vermont. His wife answered the phone and I explained who I was, and I wished to talk to her husband. She told me he was in the yard and she would find him. She put the phone down, and a little voice picked up the phone and said, "Hello." I said hello and asked her name. She said her name was Amy. I asked her how old she was, and she said, "Seven." She asked me my name but did not ask my age. I told her my name was Ron and I worked for the U.S. Senate. I asked her if she knew what the US Senate was. She told me she thought so! I asked, "What is the U.S. Senate?" She said, "Isn't that the place where they mix manure and water." I told her she was a very bright little girl. She said good-bye, and her father took the phone. Her father and I had an enjoyable conversation, but not as enjoyable as my conversation with Amy. After I was done, I wrote a note to Senator Leahy and told him the story of Amy. He laughed, and I thought to myself, Amy knows more about the U.S. Senate than many senators.

MAN WITH A PLAN

FRED was a retired farmer from the small town of Chelsea, Vermont who was elected in the Republican primary to run against Senator Pat Leahy in 1992. Fred beat a well-oiled opponent and caused a sensation in the debates when he asked the opponent the number of teats on a cow… the opponent responded, "Three," and it was all over. When asked why he was running, he said because he needed the money. When told how much a senator received, he said, "All the more reason." They made a movie about Fred and his campaign called *A Man with A Plan.*

I WOULD ALSO DUMP MILK?

IT was the campaign of 1986, and Pat Leahy was running for the Senate. I was his agricultural aide helping him with agriculture in Washington and Vermont. Pat scheduled a meeting of farmers at the UVM farm barn in which Senator Tom Harkin was to speak. It was again one of those difficult times for Vermont dairy farmers, and I was left to brief Senator Harkin on what to say. My brother had worked with Tom on the House Agriculture Committee and told me Tom could often be his own man, even after being briefed. At that time, farmers were dumping milk on the state house lawn as a means of protest, and I was to tell Tom that whatever he said he was not to say he supported the dumping of milk. Tom appeared in all his fanfare, and the first thing he said, "If I was a farmer in Vermont and facing these prices, I would be dumping milk on the state house lawn!"

THE DAIRY LOBBYIST

FRANK was a dairy lobbyist for a large southeastern dairy cooperative. To those of us who knew him, he presented himself as the bagman. He followed the dairy legislation closely and was always spouting the position of the National Dairy Federation or his cooperative. I was negotiating for the senator with other Senate staff members, and the position was contrary to the cooperative's. Frank informed me if the senator did not change his position there would be no campaign funds during his next re-election. I told Frank the senator would stand on his position and I would not lower myself to even carry his message to the senator. I was so angry I told him I or the senator's other staff members never wanted to hear such threats from him or his cooperative again!

Several years passed, and I was helping my brother campaign for a seat in the Vermont legislature. One of his female campaign volunteers was discussing her travels and experiences in her early twenties. She told me she was traveling in Rome in the 1970s and met a gentleman who had worked as a front man for Bobby Kennedy and was also working for the dairy community. I asked her his name, since I knew many in the industry.

She told me I would not know him, but his name was Frank. I laughed and told her about how my brother and I knew Frank.

SUBSIDIES ONLY TO TRUE FAMILY FARMERS

AT the time of the farm bill debate in the mid-1980s, the government costs for farm supports was approximately $20 billion. It was considered a large amount but is small compared to today's costs of farm supports. The U.S. Senate Committee, chaired by Senator Jesse Helms, began their discussions by agreeing they needed to form a farm bill reducing government costs. I remember Chairman Helms asking the members if they all agreed costs should be reduced. To a member, they voiced their agreement. Then he asked if they had any ideas as to how they might reduce those costs. The majority voiced their support to provisions limiting support to "family farms." There was then a discussion as to what might and what might not be considered a "family farm." There were many varieties of farms considered "family farms." The senator then asked if any senator would agree to develop language for the farm bill that would define "family farm." No one volunteered, and it was decided they would develop a farm bill as they had in the past, and the goal of reducing government costs was abandoned.

DON'T TELL ME WHAT I'M VOTING FOR!

DURING the debate on the farm bill in the U.S. Senate, President Reagan was president, and the administration had indicated they would not support the dairy provisions of the farm bill which established a support level. The administration wanted a lower support level which would be destructive to Vermont and New England farmers. The vote on the dairy provision promised to be close, and Senator Leahy was lining up all the support he could. The administration knew it would be close and sent Vice President Bush to the Senate to break a possible tie. Senator Leahy went to Senator Goldwater and asked if he could have his vote in support of the dairy provisions. Senators often voted for provisions with little impact on their state in exchange for votes elsewhere. Goldwater told Leahy he could have his vote, but if Leahy tried to tell him what it was for or explain the provision, he, Goldwater, would vote against it! The dairy provision passed by one vote. Perhaps, the Goldwater's vote.

YOU CAN RIDE BACK TO VERMONT IN THEIR PLANE

MY twin brother and the rest of his equals throughout the country were lobbying Congress to save the Farm Credit System. Some of the systems in other parts of the country had issued faulty farm loans, and the debt was threatening to destroy the entire system. Roger was working for the New England Farm Credit System located in Springfield, Massachusetts which served all New England farmers. He scheduled a time when he and the president of the system could visit Senator Leahy in Washington. As his agricultural advisor, I was invited to the meeting. I was aware the system owned their own plane and hired pilots, rather than using commercial airlines. Roger felt it was imprudent for them to ask for aid to "bail out the system" while at the same time traveling in a private plane. However, he could do nothing about the situation. They were meeting with the senator and asking him to support the bill rescuing the system. After they made the request and before they exited, I suggested perhaps the next time they came down and went back to New England they could give the senator a ride in their private plane. With that statement, the senator said, "You have a private plane." They sheepishly said they did but were about to sell the plane. So, I made my brother's day... helping him get the system to do what they should have done before requesting aid.

WHAT ARE YOU GOING TO TELL THE SENATOR?

WHEN I was working for Senator Leahy, I would attend dairy and other agricultural meetings in Vermont. I attended one dairy farmer meeting in Addison County during one of those difficult dairy-farming times. The farmers were quite unruly, and after I made my presentation, they asked me what I was going to tell the senator. I told them I was going to tell Senator Leahy they had not changed; they could not agree on anything.

MEADOWLARK LEMON

JESSIE Helms was chairman of the Senate Agricultural Committee. Jessie was a North Carolina senator who was reputed to be against the civil rights legislation. In committee, he was always civil and pleasant to all who testified or staffed the committee. One day during hearings, a large African American walked in and sat in front of me. I was astounded by the size of the person and thought I had seen him before. As a child, I had watched the Harlem Globetrotters, and the man looked familiar. The chairman called for a pause in the hearing so he could introduce his dear friend. He announced, "I would like to introduce my dear friend from North Carolina, Meadowlark Lemon, a former member of the Harlem Globetrotters." Meadowlark stood for applause, and as he sat down, I leaned over to shake his hand. My small hand was about one-quarter the size of his hand. I then understood how he could hold a basketball with one hand!

Farm Service Agency

WE DON'T DELIVER MAIL WHEN IT RAINS!

PRESIDENT Clinton appointed me as Director of the Farm Service Agency serving Vermont and the Virgin Islands. I thought it would be a good experience as my only connection to the islands occurred when I was on the U.S.S. *America* on the way to Vietnam. We had anchored so the admiral and captain could go ashore and play golf. The crew was restricted to the ship and could only gawk at the shore. My first visit to the islands was an eye opener, for I saw that their timeline for performing and their social system was much different than ours. The system seemed to work on relationships and payoffs. I asked one of the young people who had moved to the islands from the states what surprised him the most. He said on rainy days the mail, delivered by the U.S. Postal System, was often not delivered. He asked why and was told they didn't deliver on rainy days! Most of the island's agriculture was made up of small plots less than an acre. The agricultural department in the islands had been given jurisdiction over an old sugar cane plantation and could lease the land to people wishing to produce products. As there were sufficient loan funds for new farmers, I inquired why so little of the land had been leased. Was it because no one wanted to farm? I shortly discovered it was related to the politics of the island… who you knew and were connected to was important. It was not long before Washington removed the islands from Vermont's jurisdiction and moved it to Florida. It cost the U.S. government millions of dollars to provide small amounts of farm aid to an island really not in need of such aid.

MAROONED IN A PLANE

PAT was a farmer friend who farmed in West Danville, Vermont and who served as a long-term president of the Cabot Cooperative. Pat served many years as chairperson of the board when Cabot was a small independent cooperative. He was a true Vermonter who carried jokes in every pocket and talked with a distinctive Northern Vermont accent. As a dairy leader, the politicians were often appointing Pat to various boards, seeking his advice, and inviting him to testify at various forums. Pat was appointed as chairperson of the Farm Service Agency State Board while I was serving as its director. The three members of the state committee and myself were called to Washington to attend one of the many events. We flew on a small aircraft out of Burlington, Vermont and landed at Washington (Reagan) Airport. It was one of those commuter airlines which parked on the tarmac and bussed its flyers to the terminal. Pat and I were sitting in the back of the airline near the restroom. The airplane parked, and as I was sitting in the aisle seat, I deplaned before Pat and hopped into the second bus, assuming Pat had also deplaned and had loaded into the first bus. We reached the terminal, and as I approached the two other state committee members, I asked for Pat. They told me they had not seen Pat. I went to the counter and told them we were missing a flyer from the flight. They told me everyone was off the plane and we could not be missing a passenger. A few minutes later, they announced Pat had been found, and he was on his way to the terminal. When the plane landed and parked, Pat had gone to the restroom. The plane was cleared, and all the doors were shut with Pat left in the plane. Pat went to the cockpit and was knocking on the window when someone noticed and he was let off the plane. Pat had his own plane all to himself.

SHE WAS A REAL WITCH

AS director of the Vermont Farm Service Agency, I oversaw nine county offices in Vermont. The supervisor of the county offices came back one day after hiring a person for a northern office. He reported he was pleased with the person and as an aside said she was a registered witch. I told him there was one person in an office who admitted being a witch!

READING MY PAPERS

THE Vermont's Farm Service Agency, a part of USDA, provides disaster relief and financing to Vermont farmers. One of my employees would arrive before 7:00 a.m. and was reading the material on my desk before I arrived around 7:30 a.m. Disasters were occurring in the Midwest and some states were being asked to temporarily assign personnel to those states to assist. I decided to have a little fun. After he left for the day, I placed a notice on my bulletin board signifying we were temporarily assigning a person from Vermont to North Dakota for four weeks. I then prepared a letter to the person involved assigning him to North Dakota for four weeks and left it open on my desk. When I came in the next morning, he was on the phone to his wife informing her he would be in North Dakota for four weeks. I waited until midday to tell him the truth. When I told him he smiled and said, "you really got me."

OUR FURNITURE

I visited a hardwood furniture factory in Morrisville, Vermont. I marveled at the technological changes which had taken place since my youth in my father's lumber and chair sawmill. The mill was totally automated, and I was astonished at the furniture produced under automated conditions. I asked the manager about the nature of his competition. He invited me to a back room with Maple furniture on display. He said, "See that furniture? It is made in China, and we can import that furniture cheaper than we can buy the logs going into this plant!"

WHERE IS CONGRESSMAN SANDERS?

NORTHERN Vermont suffered a damaging ice storm, knocking out power, and doing damage to property. I was invited to tour part of the damage with Senator Leahy and Senator Jeffords. We were all crammed into a large van, the senators, their staff, the adjutant general, and me. I asked one of the senator's staff why Congressman Sanders was not with us. She said he was not asked! Sanders had yet to elevate himself to a respectable position within the Vermont/Washington community.

MORALE

I was on the job as director for the Vermont Farm Service Agency for approximately two weeks. One of the young staffers came to my office and said, "Mr. Allbee, the morale in the Vermont agency is terrible, what are you going to do about it?" When staff indicates morale is terrible, it means they want something. I told her the story about General Marshall for whom the Marshall Plan, which remade Western Europe, was named. General Marshall was head of the war department. An aide came in and said, "General Marshall, the morale is terrible out there, what are you going to do about it?" General Marshall replied, "Who in hell is taking care of my morale?"

FIRST COUNTRY VISITED BY A U.S. PRESIDENT

I often attended meetings in Washington, D.C. My peer in New Hampshire also attended those meetings. At every meeting, they would ask us to stand and identify ourselves as well as the state we represented. The New Hampshire fellow would stand and tell everyone he represented the state with the first primary election for president in the nation. After hearing him say that at several meetings, I decided to one up him. At the next meeting I told the assembly I represented Vermont; the first foreign country visited by a U.S. President. Vermont was a republic before it became a state and was visited by George Washington when he served as president.

CHAPTER 13

MEDICINE

MANURE TO MEDICINE

IN 2004, I moved with my wife and stepdaughter to Florida to help start a medical practice. I also helped a cardiologist friend start his medical practice. Although there were differences in many aspects of medical, I found the business principles were the same. After several years, I joked with people and said with my agricultural business and medical business experiences I was going to write a book called "From Manure to Medicine." My twin brother Roger followed me and became acting CEO of a small Vermont hospital and saw that side of the medical equation. Like me, he spent several years in the agricultural business and regulatory field. Thus, we are both going to join and write a book called "From Manure to Medicine." The similarities are intriguing… less than free market, difficult to understand the pricing mechanism, utilization of new technologies, heavily regulated, imperfect consumer knowledge. What is good for the industry may not be good for practitioners and vice versa, specialization versus generalization, and making it difficult for the public to understand.

AM I GOING TO MAKE MY PROBATION?

THE medical practice I managed provided a ninety-day probationary period for all new hires. During that time an employee could be discharged without reason, and they were also ineligible for benefits. I hired a young British woman who had moved to the states. She kept asking me if she was going to make the probationary period. I finally told her it was highly unlikely she would make the cut. She wondered why; if she was perform-ing well, she should make probation. I told her my mother's name was Woodbury. The Woodbury's' were estate owners in England in the 1300s, and they were related through marriage to Anne Boleyn. They backed the wrong king, and their estates were taken and several lost their heads. How could I in good conscience approve the continuation of a person representing a country which had cut the heads off my relatives! We all laughed, and the of her probation was approved.

I AM AN ASSHOLE

MY stepdaughter had been operating her dermatology practice for about a year. All new patients were required to provide their social security numbers so we could file their insurance claim. One day, one of the patients was refusing to provide his social security number, and the front desk asked me to come and talk to him. The gentleman told me he had retired as a vice president of a large health insurance company and was familiar with the requirements. He knew we could not request his Medicare number. He further told me he was "an asshole." I told him he was the first honest person I had met that day! My humor caused him to calm down and provide his Medicare number.

YOU MUST HIRE HER

MY wife has a warm heart and is always trying to help other people, particularly those who are looking for employment. Susan was seeing a physical downsizing rehab practice. She asked me to interview and hire their financial person at SkinSmart Dermatology. I interviewed the woman and told her to come in to work on a certain day. On the appointed day, she showed up to work and started talking to her housing contractor. I instructed her to go home, take care of her problem, and return the next day. She did show up the next day, and she started telling the front desk staff and the billing staff how to perform their jobs. It did not take long before the existing staff told me either they were leaving, or I could discharge the new employee. I called the person into my office and told her it was not working out, and she could leave immediately. A few months later, she was angry at her discharge from another practice and walked in with a gun and killed the practice manager. She later returned home and committed suicide. She might have shot me.

IS DOCTOR ALLBEE IN?

I was managing my stepdaughter's dermatology practice in Florida. A new young receptionist was manning the telephone when my twin brother called from Vermont. He asked to speak to Dr. Allbee. She informed him there was no Dr. Allbee at the practice. He said there was because a Dr. Allbee operated on him the previous day. It really freaked the poor girl out!

WHY CAN'T PEOPLE UNDERSTAND THEIR INSURANCE?

CHRIS was in charge of coding and billing for the medical practice. One day she came to me and said she was tired of people calling about their health insurance policies. She asked, "Why can't people understand their health insurance policies?" While I was sympathetic, I asked her how could we expect them to understand their insurance policies when we often did not understand their policies? She admitted I was correct and walked away.

SPIRIT IN A PATIENT'S ROOM

MY 100-year-old friend died in Essex, N.Y. and I moved her diaries to Florida. She maintained diaries during the many years of her life, some going back to her high school and college years in the early 20th century. I read some of the entries and found they mainly dealt with her social life. She was a private person, and although she left no directions to destroy the diaries, I knew she would not like them read or published. I found an empty room in the medical practice to store them. One evening, Sharon, the cleaning person, approached me and said she and others were afraid when they neared one of the rooms. She said everyone would sense energy, and the hair on their arms would stand up on end. She did not know what was causing the energy force but asked me to accompany her to the room. I surmised it might be the room with the diaries, and sure enough, it was the room . The next day I removed one of the diaries and asked one of the employees who claimed to be clairvoyant to hold the diary. She immediately dropped the diary and said whomever it was wanted the diaries destroyed and was not happy. Shortly thereafter, I moved the diaries to my residence where I oversaw their destruction.

HOME BAPTIST

JOHNNY was one of our cleaners in the medical practice in Sarasota. Johnny cleaned at nights and worked construction during the days. One evening, I asked Johnny if he ever took time off from his work. He told me Sundays were his free day, and he spent the entire day at church. He said he was a Southern Baptist and invited me to go to his church. I told him I was also a Baptist, but a Vermont home Baptist. He said he had never heard of a home Baptist. I said it was very similar to his church. He asked me how it differed. I told him we baptized ourselves in the home bathtub once per week.

HEART DOCTORS EAT THEIR OWN

DURING my ten years in medicine, I helped a dermatologist and a heart doctor start and market their practices. I learned much about how doctors acted, particularly how they interacted with their own kind. Much of it was based on their source of patients. Surgical dermatologists receive many referrals from other doctors… their other patients come from advertising and patient referrals. Heart doctors, because they have a stronger tie to the hospitals and the hospital referral network, seem to be more competitive. I told one heart doctor that they, as a profession, were like the praying mantis. He asked me what I meant. I said heart doctors eat their own. He agreed with my characterization.

PREPONDERANCE OF EVIDENCE

THE recent exposé of sexual harassment reminds me of a situation when I managed a cardiology practice. I hired a man with medical management experience as an operations manager. One day, a very young lady came to me and said whenever he walked into her office he would come over, rub her shoulders, and stroke her hair. I asked if he also did the same to other women in the office. She said yes, and I talked to other women who said the same. I immediately informed the doctor and said we needed to curtail his employment. The employee manual detailed harassment, and all employees received a copy they signed. So, the doctor and I met with the employee, and I asked if what was alleged was true. He said it was and he did not intend any harm. I asked if he understood harassment as defined in the manual. He said he did. So, I directed him to immediately remove his items and leave the premises. He filed for unemployment, and a hearing was held where the women testified to his actions, which he did not deny. The finding was in favor of the employer. He appealed, and another appeal hearing was held. Again, everyone testified. The appeal officer decided in favor of the employee and found "there was not a preponderance of evidence." I later found the state had a tendency to favor the employees so the employer would be charged for the unemployment. So, I learned what the term "preponderance of evidence" means when you have all the evidence and it is ignored by the appeals officer.

HOW LONG DOES IT TAKE YOU TO PUT A STENT IN?

I was helping a heart doctor start his practice in Sarasota when I suffered heart seizures. He reviewed my problem and told me he would place some stents in my heart the following day. I asked him how long it would take him to install the two stents. He told me he could perform the procedure in five minutes. The next day as the nurses were preparing me, I asked if they had a stopwatch. They asked why it was important. I told them I wanted them to time the doctor to see if he could perform the procedure in five minutes.

WHAT YOU SHOULD EAT

A few years ago, I started having chest pains. I called my heart doctor who I was helping, and he suggested I immediately go to the emergency room. I did so, and after some review, they told me I was just having indigestion. Fortunately, my doctor friend arrived and read the EKG and decided to place two stents in my heart. As I was later reviewing my health with him, he recommended several eating habits. I had grown up on cheese and milk, and he recommended I curtail my cheese consumption and drink low fat or nonfat milk. Fortunately, red wine consumption was considered advisable in moderation. He said, "If it walks on four, don't eat it, and if it walks on two, you shouldn't eat it!" That has been the philosophy I have employed, and my health is considerably better.

KEEP YOUR EYE ON THE BIRD!

I was employed to help a cardiologist friend start his medical practice. He had already purchased a site, and it was being built out to meet his needs. Meanwhile, he was working out of another office and we started hiring staff, purchasing equipment, and otherwise preparing for a start-up. Early one morning, I received an email from the cardiologist asking me if he should take a temporary position in Sebring, several miles away from Sarasota. I told him he was starting a practice (business), and it was important for him to "keep his eye on the bird," and the bird was not in Sebring. He took my advice.

TOO MUCH SILICONE

MY stepdaughter decided to visit a business with spray tanning. Since I was riding with her, I also decided on a spray tan. As I walked into the business, the front counter woman was quite noticeable. Her breast was so enlarged with silicone they hung over the counter. I must admit, she was very attractive and the large breast did not hinder her beauty. Signing in, I asked if it would be safe for me to enter the booth? I wondered if I would receive more than a tan! I did not want big boobs!

CHAPTER 14

MISCELLANOUS

PURE MAPLE SYRUP IN PRAGUE

MY twin brother and his partner were exporting cranberries to Europe. They traveled to food shows throughout Europe and were staying at a fancy hotel in Prague. Pancakes with pure Maple syrup were on the breakfast menu. Roger ordered the pancakes and Maple syrup. It was evident the syrup was not pure Maple, but a sugary blend. Roger asked to speak to the chef who was American. Roger told him it was not Maple syrup, but a concocted blend. The chef said it was evident Roger knew it, the chef knew it, but nobody in Prague would know it!

ROGER AND ANN AND A DOG IN BED

MY twin brother and his wife Ann owned a black Labrador dog named Cleo. Cleo often slept in their bed at night. One morning, Ann awoke, and Cleo was between them with her head on their pillow. Ann told my brother they had to do something about the dog in their bed. My brother responded, "Ann, you are not going to make me choose between the dog and you?" Cleo started sleeping on the floor!

COLOSTOMY AND WHAT TO SAY BEFORE THEY TAKE YOU AWAY

I was at the University of Vermont Health Center in Burlington being prepared for a colostomy. I laid in the prep room with other patients and watched as they were rolled into the procedure room. When my time came, the nurse asked if I had anything I wished to say before the procedure. I told her I did. I said I wanted to know what would happen. I witnessed all the patients being wheeled out for the procedure and none came back! She told me I was the only patient who noticed and assured me I would come back!

NEWFANE COMMON

THE Newfane common is a very picturesque site with a common and the Greek-style courthouse. The common was donated to the county by my great-great-grandfather Park who was a Revolutionary War veteran of the Battle of Bennington and bestowed much to the town of Newfane. Prior to the 1970s, county government in Vermont was reduced with the establishment of the district-style government. Lieutenant Governor Burgess, recognizing the reduced status of the counties, submitted legislation to turn the common over to the district. He was stymied in his attempt because a clause in the deed stated should the county be removed from ownership; the property would revert to the heirs. We figured my family would receive a few square yards of the common. Of course, we did not want the common, but I did desire that softball return to the common. The town had prohibited softball and other sports on the common, which was a blemish on the town's record. I have been encouraging my cousin Howard, also a relative of the donator, to bring one of his cows to the common during the annual heritage festival so there can again be cow shit on the common. Commons were originally established as a place for area farmers to bring animals. Thus, the name common.

SONS OF AMERICAN REVOLUTION MEETING

MY twin brother began the process for becoming members of the Sons of the American Revolution. We had to prove our ancestors on both my mother's and father's side of the family fought in the American Revolution. It was not hard for us to find the information on both sides of the family. I went to my first Vermont meeting in Montpelier, Vermont and met a few people. I found it entertaining when they announced their efforts to stand by the constitution. All I was thinking about our dysfunctional government in Washington and wondering what my ancestors would think about the current Congress, runaway budgets, large defense spending, etc. If they were alive today would they start another revolution?

CHASING WHAT YOU EAT

I am an avid fly fisherman and historically, have been an avid bird hunter. Very infrequently do I play golf, tennis, or other such sports. In Florida, people asked if I played golf. I always told them I did not chase anything I could not eat!

ARE YOU A NATIVE?

I don't know why it matters, but I was always asked if I was a native Vermonter. My brother was serving as Vermont's secretary of agriculture, and he was asked by the then fish and game commissioner if he was a native. The person told him he was, and his family was in Vermont at the time of the French and Indian War. Roger told him his family came a few years before the Revolutionary War and the fish and game commissioner's family undoubtedly cleaned our houses!

NOTHING RUNS LIKE A DEERE

JOHN Deere was a native of Addison County, Vermont. If you visit Middlebury, Vermont today, you will see a sign commemorating the home of John Deere. If you read the history of Vermont and John Deere, you will learn he was a blacksmith whose tools were sought by local farmers. However, financially, he was less successful. Due to his difficult finances, he left Vermont and his family and moved West, eventually moving his family with him. He found success in the West developing a plow that was revolutionary for its time. However, because he left Vermont and his debts, we would kiddingly tell people that "nothing runs like a Deere" came from his leaving Vermont under less than ideal conditions.

THEY DID NOT READ THE BOOK

ONE of the more unfortunate events in Vermont was the eugenics movement. The University of Vermont was a leading researcher on eugenics, or the better breeding of the human race. One professor even wrote a book called, *How to Breed a Better Vermonter*. I would tell doctors I understood the reason for my health problems ,and they would inquisitively ask me what it was. I would tell them my parents failed to read a book called *How to Breed Better Vermonters!*

WAIT AND THERE WILL BE MORE COWS

ONE morning, a young man was driving by a farm early, and he noted that a farm cow was out in the road. He stopped at the farm, knocked on the door, and told the farmer one of his cows was out in the road. The farmer thanked him and said if he waited a little longer there would be more cows out in the road.

THE GENERAL WHO DISAPPEARED

IN the early 2000, my wife and I owned a condo on Spear Street in Burlington, Vermont. The area was known as Overlake, and I liked to say that they would do a picture calendar of the women of Overlake called "Overlooked at Overlake." We liked to refer to it as the weigh station for the senior housing in Shelburne. One of the condos was owned by a Venezuelan general and his family and had been used infrequently during the years. At some point, the general stopped paying both his condo fees and his property taxes on the condo. The city started the process to sell the property for taxes, and the condo association started the process to pay the taxes and take over the condo. Searches were made to find both the general and his family to no avail. He and his family had simply disappeared. The association found itself owning a condo completely full of everything from toys to art to a car. Every conceivable item a person could buy was in the condo. The association placed a price on the condo contents. I and another person purchased the items and started the process of inventorying and selling the items. The most interesting item I found was a complete notebook full of notes from the hearing of Clinton's impeachment and the general's notes of the proceedings. The general's pictures together with all of his medals were also in the apartment. I concluded he became involved with the CIA and they placed him and his family in a different area with totally different names and backgrounds.

FISHING GRASSY BROOK

WHEN growing up in Brookline, Vermont, Grassy Brook flowed the entire length of the town and was a premier trout stream. Brown trout traveled up the stream from the West River, and the stream was home to a wonderful population of brook trout. The stream was fed by a series of springs in the north end of town. A few years ago, I thought I might again try my hand at fishing Grassey. I noted it no longer flowed steady in the summer, and many of the springs feeding the stream had been cut off by housing developments. I fished the entire length of the stream and caught one trout and saw many dace and suckers. Where there was once abundance, there was now nothing. It was truly a death of a once vibrant stream.

THE VIETNAM OFFICER WHO HATED THE CHINESE

MY brother was running the Vermont Farm Service Agency, and the man who cleaned served in the South Vietnamese Army as a major. After the fall of South Vietnam, he was sent to rehabilitation working in the jungles and surviving on what little he could find to eat. Finally, he was allowed to immigrate to the U.S. to join his family. Roger was talking to him one evening, and he was telling Roger how much he hated the Chinese. It goes back many centuries. He told Roger he would not purchase any product produced in China. Roger asked him to remove his shoes and look at where they were produced. He did so and saw China was on label. He replied, "I will throw out these shoes, they are no good!"

SEND HER HOME!

IN the 1990s, my wife served as the overseer of approximately thirty au pairs. She would place them with families, oversee their needs, and if necessary, remove them from the homes. Some families treated the young people as part of their family, and others took advantage of the person. My wife placed one young girl with a doctor and his family. It was his second marriage, and his young stepson lived in a separate part of the house. Either the young man needed more attention from the au pair, or the au pair found him needing attention. Either way, they became a couple in the house. The father threatened to sue the company. The au pair was removed, and a payment was made to the family. A little later, the stepfather paid for the young lady to return to the U.S. to spend time with his stepson. Perhaps, the payment helped with the return passage.

YOU MIGHT HAVE BEEN A CARDINAL

TWO of the people my wife and I introduced were married in Spain. Montse who was Spanish planned a wedding in her hometown of Ponferada, Spain. Several people from Vermont, including me and my wife, traveled to Spain to attend the wedding. One of the wedding guests from Vermont was a UVM Spanish professor and a friend of the bride. It was a wonderful wedding with a dinner starting around 11 p.m. that evening. Several courses were served accompanied by wine... all you could drink or eat. After the desserts, grappa of several varieties was served. We were all very happy and well-lubricated by the end of the evening. The monsignor, who was a boyhood friend of the father of the bride, stayed until the end and enjoyed the libations. As he was leaving, he came to our table to wish us the best and say good-bye. Not too long before the wedding, Pope Benedict was appointed, and the news reported that he had been a member of the Nazi youth organization growing up in Germany. The UVM Spanish professor wished him goodbye, thanked him, and told him in Spanish, "If the pope wasn't a Nazi, you would be a cardinal by now!" The monsignor hardly noticed but did smile and gave us his blessing.

HOW MY FRIEND MOWED LAWNS FOR HIS FATHER

ONE of my fly-fishing friends told me about his experience working for his father who was a very successful businessman in the south. Tom was told it was time for him to start working during his summer vacation. He was to mow the lawns around the lumber business. On the first day, he was given a lawn mower with a two-cycle engine. Such engines require oil added to the fuel to maintain proper functioning. Tom was not aware of the requirement, and the engine froze. The next day, he was given another lawn mower, and he was mowing a bank when the mower broke loose, traveled across the highway, and smashed into a brick wall. The third day, he was provided a tractor with a mower cutter attached. Somehow, the blade broke free from the mower and flew through a parked car. On the fourth day, they decided that power equipment was not safe around Tom and gave him a stick with a cutter attached that he could swing at the grass. He came upon a hornet's nest in the grass. He remembered gasoline, when ignited, was a good tonic for hornets and their nests. Tom grabbed five gallons of gas and threw it on the hornet's nest igniting the gas. Suddenly, he had a grass fire out of control headed to the lumberyard. It was a three-alarm fire. It was the end of his grass cutting career.

BUFFALO IN THE STREAM

I love fly-fishing and not because I am anxious to catch fish. I am just as happy when I do not catch fish. It is my chance to become one with nature. One year, I traveled with my stepdaughter to Wyoming to attend a medical conference. My excuse for going was to carry her bags and my fly-fishing equipment. I was directed to a wildlife reservation where a stream with golden trout passed through the reservation. I fished up the stream catching several trout. After I had fished about a mile upstream, I decided to turn around and fish down the stream. After fishing a few minutes down the stream, I looked up and saw two large beasts standing in the stream directly in my path. There were two buffalo, a mother and its young. I decided to exit the stream and give the wildlife that owned the stream a free pass.

POPE FRANCIS AND QUEEN ELIZABETH

A few weeks after the queen was visiting the pope in Italy, I was joking with a couple of employees about some of the things the pope and Queen Elizabeth might have said to each other. The queen probably asked the pope why she could not wear white and he could. She might also have marveled at his hat and wished she could wear such a small hat rather than the larger hats she was always seen wearing. She probably asked him who designed his outfits. The pope, on the other hand, probably asked when he could get the Church of England back.

VERNON FARMER AND HIS STOCK

AN investment advisor trying to sell stocks visited one of my very successful Vernon, Vermont farmers. He inquired if the farmer had stock. The farmer replied he had a couple hundred stock, and some days they are up, and some days they are down. He wasn't about to purchase any additional stock. It took the advisor a few seconds to comprehend he was talking about his cattle.

PAINTING CARS

A friend in Barre and I both drove cars with too much salt damage. During winter, the roads were salted which caused damage to vehicles, and our vehicles showed a little body damage. Fred possessed all the equipment necessary to paint the automobiles. I grew up helping my father repair rusted vehicles. We decided to help each other repair and paint the vehicles. We worked several weekends filling and sanding the autos and then masking and taping the parts we did not want painted. The final products looked almost professional, and the previous scars were undetectable. I did not know Fred was going to sell his vehicle after our work. About two weeks following the repairs, a neighbor drove in with a very nice-looking Volkswagen station wagon. He was proud of his recently purchased vehicle and showed it to me with some pride. I did not tell him it was Fred's vehicle we recently patched and painted!

CAN I HELP WITH YOUR TAXES?

MY friend in Essex, New York who I helped care for was trying to complete her own federal taxes. I would visit and see her with the tax forms and offer to help. She informed me she was capable of completing her own taxes. When she finally was unable to handle her own financial affairs, I started looking for her past tax submissions. Although she did not have an income which would have required a payment, filing was a requirement. I finally asked her where her past filed forms were, and she responded she had not filed for the past couple of years. I told her it was a requirement, and she could be fined. She responded, "What are they going to do, put me

in a white-collar jail!" When she died, we sorted everything out v..
IRS, and there was no payment due.

BOSTON RED SOX

MY son and daughter-in-law were traveling to California from Vermont when the Red Sox and Yankees were playing in the World Series. My daughter-in-law and family are die-hard Red Sox fans from the Boston area. They were dressed in Red Sox hats and shirts as they were traveling. Their plane stopped in New York, and they had to change planes and again go through security. As they were passing through security, they were pulled aside and asked to go into a separate room. My son was beside himself because they had done nothing wrong. The TSA person escorted them to a room full of people watching the game on TV. He said that he needed some more Red Sox fans to help even out the support for the teams.

GETTING BEYOND THE DOOR GUARD!

AFTER high school, my son traveled to Arizona and spent two years living ten miles in the Roosevelt Mountains studying herbs. He lived in a yurt over a rattlesnake den. He returned to Vermont in January and said he was ready to go to college. David had been an excellent student in high school and graduated in the top ten in his class. When he came back to Vermont, I suggested we visit the admitting department at the university. I knew it would be interesting because it was a little late to be enrolling in the spring semester. UVM had just stated in the paper they were seeking good Vermont students. We entered the building, and I went with David to the front desk. The woman at the front desk took her job seriously and immediately informed David it was too late to enroll in the spring semester. He would have to wait and enroll in the fall. I recognized her as a door guard and knew door guards, if approached properly, can always find an exception. At last resort, I would call my friend Tom Salmon who was serving as president of the university... but that would be last resort. I told the woman I had three questions for her: 1. was UVM looking for good students, 2. were they looking for exceptional Vermont students and 3. had the classes started yet? Finally, she said that we could talk to a counselor... the door was opened. The counselor was very positive, and as a result,

David was admitted for the spring semester. He went on to graduate Phi Beta Kappa!

CAT TRACKS ON A BIRTHDAY CAKE

THE Perry's in Windham, Vermont were an interesting Vermont farm couple. He was a very intelligent and neat farmer and by walking through the farm you could see that he was an excellent manager. She, a kind but obviously challenged wife, had a difficult time keeping house, and it never looked like she cleaned. She had a kind heart. Prior to owning the farm in Windham, they were farm managers for the Knapp family in Brookline, Vermont. Stanley was the owner's young son, and his mother was not a woman allegedly with the warmest of hearts. Stanley tells the story of Mabel making him a birthday cake with cat tracks across the frosting. Stanley, realizing it came from the heart, ate his piece of cake. Stanley would stay a close friend of the Perry family all his life.

ESTABLISHING A REPUTATION

THE University of Vermont was known as a party school, and when a new resident, Judith Ramalle was hired, she made it a priority to end the reputation of the university for partying. She traveled to Southern Vermont where she met with a delegation of Vermont graduates. Jack Burgess served as lieutenant governor of Vermont and was a resident of Brattleboro as well as a graduate of the university. The president made her presentation before the UVM area alumni, and after she was finished, Lieutenant Governor Burgess said, "Pardon me, Madam President, but I want you to know many of us worked hard to establish the partying and drinking reputation for the university, and we were very proud of our accomplishments!"

I KNOW WHO YOU ARE

IT was the early 1970s, and my stepson was manning the register at my food store in South Burlington. We were not taking credit cards at the register but were using them for shipping and ordering of gift packages. I noticed a tall gentleman at the register with an armful of wine. He was asking my stepson if we accepted credit cards, and my stepson was telling him we did not. I approached the register and told the person we would take his credit card. He said he had identification and would be most happy to provide it for my review. I said I did not need it as I recognized him. He laughed and started asking me about the store and some of the Tibetan flags we had hanging in the store. He was quite pleasant. When he left and we helped him to his car with a case of wine, I told my stepson it was Peter Jennings, the national journalist.

THE SCOTS AMONG US

IN the 1960s, two retired doctors of Scottish ancestry retired to Brookline and Newfane area. They came from a family of sheep farmers in Montana. One was a retired veterinarian and the other a retired surgeon. They both purchased hillside farms where they raised sheep, they herded with trained border collies. The vet was gregarious, outgoing and just loved visiting with people. He joined the fire department and contributed to community activities. His brother, the surgeon, was more reclusive and did not integrate himself into the community. He was also very conservative, something his brother never let him forget. He would go to my uncle's restaurant, and rather than order a drink, he would order a half glass of water and take the cream picture and dump it into his glass. It was his way of having a glass of non-fat milk without paying for it. One day, he was collecting the eggs from his hen house when one dropped on the driveway. He went into the house for a dish and spoon so he could save the egg! They noticed some of their sheep were being killed by a dog. Not thinking it could be their well-trained border collies, they drove around town checking the teeth of all the dogs. Later, they announced it was one of their border collies which they were forced to put down.

HOW WE COMMUNICATE

COMMUNICATION is critical in any environment. I always use the following example when discussing the difficulty of human communications with employees. My wife and I drove to Montreal one weekend. Toward the end of the stay, she asked to visit a bagel store to purchase "Montreal Bagels." I drove to the store in the northern part of the city and could not find a parking space. I double-parked and asked my wife to man the car. As I was about to leave the car, she asked that I purchase three dozen of "every kind" of bagel. I slammed the door and told her I was not about to purchase so many bagels! I purchased three dozen of three different kinds of bagels and returned to the car. She told me "every kind" was a type of bagel!

HAVING MY PAST LIFE READ BY A PSYCHIC

I helped a friend sell her aesthetics business. She was also a psychic and offered to do a past life reading on me. She told me I was always part of the sea. I told her I did serve in the U.S. Navy. No, she said, I was also a Roman sea captain. I said it was better than being a rower! She then told me I was a captain of one of Columbus's ships, the *Pinta*. I said it was probably why I liked a good Italian red wine and I really discovered America, not Columbus! I then asked about my twin brother. She told me my twin and I had many past lives together, that I was once his mother. I told her he didn't send me a Mother's Day card. I then called my brother and told him the story and said I expected Mother's Day cards in the future!

IF YOU WANT A DRINK, BRING ONE

FRED was a farmer who lived in a small village in Central Vermont. He once ran as a Republican for the U.S. Senate and they made a movie about his quest. A friend lived in the same small town and told me the following story. Fred invited a neighbor to join him at his house for a drink. He said, "come on up and have a drink, if you want one too bring a bottle!"

DUMPING MILK ON THE STATE HOUSE LAWN

WHEN milk prices were low in the 1970's farmers from the northeastern part of Vermont would bring a milk truck to Montpelier and dump milk on the State House lawn. They would notify the press of their activities. They would always call the Agriculture Department and inform them of the dumping. I suspected they would not really dump milk on the lawn and asked the lab to sample the dumping. They found the farmers were dumping lime and water on the lawn.

IT IS NOT JUST ABOUT NUTS

MY wife was a very successful entrepreneur. She started a discount cheese and food store in Burlington, Vermont. Her shopping gene is so strong she will spend hours in a store. We went on a cruise with her daughter and son in law. On the way back we were passing a Costco store and my wife asked her son in law to stop so she could purchase some nuts. I warned him it was never just about nuts. She went into the store and filled two shopping carts. There was hardly enough room in the car for her groceries. I told her son in law, "it is never just about nuts."

MEANING OF "LIVE FREE OR DIE"

WHEN I lived in Southern Vermont I often shopped in Keene, New Hampshire. One day I went to purchase a kerosene heater from a N.H. hardware store. They asked me if I was a N.H. resident. I said no and asked them why they asked. If I was a N.H. resident I needed approval from the local fired department to purchase the equipment. As a Vermont resident I did not require such a certificate. I asked the clerk what "Live Free or Die" as a N.H. memo meant.